KILLING NO MURDER
South Wales and the Great Railway Strike of 1911

Robert Griffiths

[handwritten signature]
COMMUNIST UNIVERSITY
OF BRITAIN 2009

manifesto

First published in 2009 by Manifesto Press
in association with the Rail, Maritime and Transport Union

Manifesto Press
Ruskin House
23 Coombe Road
Croydon CRO 1BD
info@manifestopress.org.uk
www.manifestopress.org.uk

Cover

*The funeral procession for John John and Leonard Worsell
in Llanelli, August 1911, after they had been shot dead
(reproduced by kind permission of Cardiff Central Library).*

Typset in ITC Garamond
Printed in Britain by North Wolds Printers Ltd

ISBN 978-1-907464-01-0

i Elin, Osian, Cei, Rhydian ac Emily a'r to sy'n codi i etifeddu'r byd

Contents

	Foreword by Bob Crow	3
	Author's forword	5
1	Railwaymen	7
2	The Baptists' Jerusalem	18
3	The Great Strike	26
4	The Shooting	41
5	A Heavy Reckoning	50
6	The Man with the Gun at His Side	59
7	Killing No Murder?	68
8	History as Class Struggle	83
	Notes	99
	Index	112
	Illustrations	118

Foreword by Bob Crow

Killing No Murder vividly highlights an important struggle in the ongoing line of march towards creating a fighting union for all rail workers.

Our ancestors in the Amalgamated Society of Railway Servants and the NUR and our members today in RMT are united in putting the labour movement adage Unity is Strength into action.

The infamous Taff Vale judgement, which deemed that strike action was effectively illegal as it was 'in restraint of trade', was defeated in 1906 with the passing of the Trades Disputes Act.

But the battle for trade union rights had only just begun. Early forms of toothless social partnership, such as the conciliation scheme foisted on the unions by the employers the following year, still needed to be defeated.

What was required was independent, democratic industrial trade unionism and that still holds true today in the face of a relentless bosses' offensive. We still have much to learn from the battles and sacrifices made by our forbearers and we can proudly carry on that fight today in defence of working men and women and their families.

Bob Crow
General Secretary
Rail, Maritime and Transport UNION
London, October 2009

Foreword

An earlier version of this book was first published in 1986, in Welsh and under the title – which should not require translation – *Streic! Streic! Streic!* This new edition corrects and extends that work, while remaining in essence an English language translation of it.

My primary motive for producing an account of the events of 1911 is explained, at least implicitly, in the course of the final chapter. I hope this book contributes, in however small a way, to the development of revolutionary political consciousness among working people and within the labour movement.

My secondary motive was also materialistic, but in the vulgar non-Marxist sense of the word. I needed the money. It was in the early 1980s that Cwmni Ffilmiau'r Nant commissioned Gareth Miles and me to research and write a television drama-documentary programme on the 1911 railway strike in south Wales. This was broadcast in 1983 as 'Y Gwrthgiliwr' and, subsequently, in English as 'The Deserter'— a reference to Private Harold Spiers (see Chapter 6). The royalties supplemented my unemployment benefit, up to a point.

My thanks must therefore go to Alun Ffred Jones of Cwmni Ffilmiau'r Nant for his interest and support; and to Richard Houdmont, Lowri Morgan, Elgan Davies and Stephen McAllister for their part in publishing the Welsh-language book of the film. I am also grateful to Dr Deian Hopkin, who supplied me so unselfishly with the then unpublished fruits of his own pioneering research, and to Desmond Spiers of Redditch who enabled me to put a face to his uncle Harold. My own research received valuable assistance from Meinir Huws (then working for Plaid Cymru in the House of Commons), Sharon Powell, Jan Warhurst and Ann Morton at the Public Record Office. The staff at the Cardiff and Llanelli central public libraries extended their usual friendly and efficient help.

Most of all, I must acknowledge the vital contributions of my friend and comrade Gareth Miles. He spent many hours discussing my original research before writing the television script, and then took on the onerous (and unpaid) task of correcting my drafts of the Welsh language edition of this book. We continue to share a commitment to what Nikolai Ostrovsky, the character in Shokolov's classic novel *Quiet Flows the Don*, called 'the finest cause in the world – the liberation of mankind'. Except that we call it Communism: 'The simplest thing, so hard to achieve' as Bertold Brecht once put it.

Robert Griffiths

Cardiff, August 2009

1. Railwaymen

The Liberal Party returned to office after the General Election of January 1906, with Sir Henry Campbell-Bannerman commanding a substantial majority in the House of Commons. The Tories had been trounced in Wales, losing every one of their six seats, while such prominent Liberals as DA Thomas, W Llewelyn Williams and David Lloyd George now took their place on the government benches. Also sitting in the new chamber were more than 50 MPs who claimed to speak for the interests of labour: men like James Keir Hardie and John Williams, together with victorious Liberal-labour ('Lib-lab') candidates such as south Wales miners' leaders William Brace, Thomas Richards and William Abraham ('Mabon').

At the hustings, many of the Liberal candidates— and even some of the Tory ones— had pledged themselves to overturn the 'Taff Vale Judgement'. Back in 1900, following a strike by some of its employees, the Taff Vale Railway company had sued the Amalgamated Society of Railway Servants (ASRS). Even though the union had not officially endorsed its members' action, the Law Lords awarded the company £23,000 from the Society's funds as compensation for lost trade. Now, early in 1906, the Liberal government adopted a bill drafted by Labour MPs and then steered it through parliament to become the Trade Disputes Act: it repealed the Taff Vale verdict, ensuring that trades unions and their members could not be sued for the commercial damage caused by a legitimate industrial dispute. [1]

Once more, Wales was in political ferment. The Liberal resurgence breathed new life into issues that had gone stale, especially when Lloyd George entered the Cabinet as president of the Board of Trade: Disestablishment of the Church of England in Wales, reforms in housing and education, temperance measures, home rule for Ireland and Wales ... all seemed possible if not inevitable.

The Rev. RJ Campbell toured the south Wales valleys in 1907, challenging conservative Nonconformity with his 'New Theology' of Christian socialism; the Independent Labour Party (ILP) evangelised in the towns and pit villages too, with its open-air rallies and socialist Sunday Schools. New branches of the ILP were formed in Carmarthen and Haverfordwest that autumn. At the same time, the party's small but pioneering Llanelli branch was venturing into the Gwendraeth valley where, as one correspondent in the weekly newspaper *Llais Llafur ('Labour Voice')* remarked:

'We trust their advent to this locality will be the commencement of a new era, the emancipation of labour'. [2] With demonstrations and strikes spreading against non-union labour, delegates from 250 unions met in Bath, in September 1907, at the annual Trades Union Congress; they called for major programmes in housing and education, and for an inquiry into a massacre perpetrated by British troops in Belfast; they condemned the House of Lords, narrow and sectional trades unionism and the strike-breaking activities of British dockers in Antwerp. Meanwhile, the campaign continued inside the Miners' Federation of Great Britain to affiliate the union to the Labour Representation Committee (which now had its own group of 'Labour' MPs in parliament); despite the enthusiastic support of the South Wales Miners Federation (but not its Lib-lab officials), a motion in favour of affiliation had been narrowly defeated in a ballot the previous year.

Many Welsh workers still held religious beliefs, although the dramatic impact of the 1905 revival was ebbing away – to the extent, indeed, that Llais Llafur could ask the question: 'Mr Evan Roberts – PA LE Y MAE EFE?' ('Mr Evan Roberts – WHERE IS HE?') [3] The answer on this occasion, in October 1907, was that he was in Switzerland; he would disappear for weeks or even months on end, with nobody noticing. Yet only a few years had elapsed since women would faint at his feet, as sinful miners wept and wailed in repentance. Nowadays, a rather different brand of missionary attracted the attention of the Welsh people and the press: Victor Grayson, the revolutionary socialist MP for Colne Valley in Yorkshire, came to Ebbw Vale, Aberdare, Tonypandy and points west with his fiery denunciation of capitalist exploitation and oppression.

Nonetheless, it was the Liberal MP for Caernarfon Boroughs, Lloyd George, who inspired the unrivalled loyalty of his Welsh compatriots. He led the crusade to clip the wings of the House of Lords; since the Liberal election victory, their Tory lordships had killed measures to reduce the influence of the Church of England in state schools, to restrict property owners to one vote only, and to prevent a large increase in the number of public houses. Now here was the Welsh Dafydd joining battle with Goliath, reviving the petty bourgeois radical tradition and offering national leadership to Welsh workers and capitalists alike. In a famous essay, George Dangerfield splendidly captures the character of Lloyd George and the temper of the times:

He represented – or seemed to represent – all those dangerous and possibly subversive opinions which Liberalism, in its grave game of progress, was forced to tolerate. He was a great vote-catcher ... when he first exploded into English politics, and angry little solicitor from an uncouth, starved district in Wales, he brought with him something alien and dangerous. He wanted the poor to inherit the earth, particularly if it was the earth of rich English landlords; and he wanted this with a sly, semi-educated passion which struck his parliamentary colleagues as being in very bad form. [4]

However, not everyone in Wales believed that Lloyd George would be the saviour of the common people. Although *Llais Llafur* – a paper for workers published in Ystalyfera – agreed that he was more of a 'Radical' than most of his fellow-Liberals, it warned its readers: 'He, like Burns, has been bought mind, body and soul by official Liberalism, for two thousand pounds a year; he is now no more than a tail, and a tail must wag according to the will and whim of its master'. [5]

That is why, the paper continued, Lloyd George had declared when opening a new underground railway in London: 'The capitalist need not fear that the Government will ever interfere, or ever had any intention of interfering, with private enterprise'. What, the correspondent asked, about the interference of Liberal and Tory governments in the running of capitalism in Belfast, Yorkshire and Wales – sending in police and troops to quell the revolt of miners and transport workers?

The Trade Disputes Act stiffened the resolve of the railwaymen to launch their biggest-ever campaign for higher wages and a shorter working week. In November 1906, the ASRS convened a special conference in Birmingham to draw up its second 'National All-Grades Programme for England and Wales'. The Society represented 70,000 of Britain's 300,000-strong labour force on the railways, and as the industry's largest union it was responding to their deepening discontent.

The railwaymen were among the lowest-paid workers in Britain's major industries, with only the farm labourers languishing beneath them. In fact, recent decades had witnessed a severe worsening of their position in the wages league: between 1886 and 1906 wage rates rose by 26 per cent in engineering, by 24 per cent in south Wales coal mines, by 23 per cent in cotton manufacturing, by 18 per cent in construction ... and by a paltry 5 per cent on the railways.

Whereas railway wages had remained stagnant during the first six years of the new century, food and other retail prices had increased by about 5 per cent; at a time when most colliers in south Wales would have been earning between 30 and 34 shillings a week, more than one-third of railwaymen received less than 20s, while only one in ten would have been on 30s or more. A porter, platelayer or general labourer at the Great Western Railway's Llanelli station, for instance, would have been rewarded with 17s for a basic 6-day, 60 hour week; a shunter would be entitled to 20s. Even the engine driver, upon whom so many lives depended, would earn little more than 28s a week – less than the average coalminer. From these miserable sums a total of 1s 2d would then be deducted for sick pay, pensions and widows' and orphans' funds – all administered by the company, naturally. In defence of their miserliness, the directors of the railway companies pointed out that employees benefited from such 'indirect advantages' as free or cut-rate travel ... and tips.

Two-thirds of rail workers toiled for at least 60 hours a week, with most of the others working 72 hours. In addition to the standard working week, overtime was often compulsory – usually at ordinary rates, sometimes unpaid. Meal-times were outside company time. In these matters, again, the railwaymen lagged behind their brothers (and some sisters) in the engineering, chemical, gas and retail industries, many of whom had already won a reduction in their working week to 54 or even 48 hours – with little or no loss of pay. Nor were there many industries more dangerous to work in than the railways: during the ten years up to 1907, no less than 5,238 railway employees had been killed and 146,767 injured in industrial accidents. [6]

Yet such carnage and deprivation existed in an industry which – for some – was prosperous and still flourishing. The amount of capital tied up in Britain's expanding railway network had grown steadily, from £860 millions in 1890 to £1,229 millions in 1905; over the same period, total receipts from freight and passenger traffic had increased from £73 millions a year to £101 millions. [7] In 1907, a not untypical year, the companies spent £30m. on wages while reaping £45m. in profits. So rich were the pickings and consequent pay-outs to shareholders, the railway companies felt it necessary to reduce the dividend rate (the distributed profits expressed as a percentage of the share capital) artificially. This was done by making a 'scrip issue' of shares to existing shareholders, free of charge. Thus the Taff Vale Railway company had 'diluted' each £100 of share capital to £250, thereby avoiding an embarrassingly high dividend rate of 18 per cent (which might have provoked demands for higher wages and lower freight charges), while still paying out the same amount of distributed profits to shareholders. [8]

This profiteering occurred in an industry riddled with waste and unnecessary duplication: for example, Britain's fifty or more railway companies retained 3,000 directors, together with general supervisors (receiving between £4,000 and £12,000 a year – in 1907!) and regional supervisors. Passenger fares and freight tariffs varied enormously from company to company and service to service; some companies paid potential rivals not to compete on particular lines; on the more lucrative routes, up to six companies would be running services – often with near-empty carriages. Not surprisingly, therefore, the running costs on Britain's railways were the highest in the world; at the same time, so were ticket prices and company profits per mile of track. |9| Not that the directors and shareholders would have been troubled too much by international comparisons – British capital dominated the railway systems of India, Egypt, Belgium, Canada, South Africa, Argentina and other countries as well.

Against this background, it is easy to understand why the ASRS National All-Grades Programme presented to the railway companies in January 1907 contained some bold demands, including:

● a standard 8-hour day for most rail employees, with a maximum 10 hours for all other grades except platelayers;
● a minimum 9 hours rest between shifts;
● a minimum rate of time-and-a-quarter for all overtime working;
● Sundays, Christmas Day and Good Friday not to be counted as ordinary days in the standard working week;
● a guaranteed working week;
● and an immediate rise of 2s a week for all men working more than an 8 hour day. [10]

The programme of the Associated Society of Locomotive Engineers and Fireman called for locomotive workers called for mileage payments and overnight allowances for long-distance footplate staff, substantial pay rises for cleaners, firemen and drivers, and an automatic line of promotion between them. [11]

True to form, eleven of the 12 major rail companies refused to meet deputations from either of the two main railway unions to discuss their claims. Most company directors had long argued that their industry was of such unique, strategic importance to nation and empire that it could only be run according to military-style discipline and procedures. Obviously, this would exclude any role for trades unionism.

Throughout the summer of 1907, the ASRS and ASLEF agitated for their programmes and, above all, for recognition by the companies. The employers persisted with their refusal to meet and negotiate; they also pleaded poverty and helplessness, on the grounds that an Act of 1894 prevented them from unilaterally raising freight charges (to fund pay increases, for example). By the beginning of September, even the renowned patience of ASRS general secretary Richard Bell was wearing thin: he announced that a strike ballot of the Amalgamated Society's membership – now swollen to 97,000 – would be held on the issue of union recognition. In the same speech, he told his audience in Manchester that: 'For himself, he abhorred strikes more than anyone; but he felt that, as in national and international disputes, so in industrial disputes, there was a time when bayonets must be fixed and shots fired'. [12]

Such remarks were uncharacteristically militant for Richard Bell. He had been criticised frequently by some railway workers for taking the Society's money in sponsorship, while voting against the union's own policies in the House of Commons. As the Lib-lab MP for Derby, he found it more comfortable to work with the Liberals than with the new Parliamentary Labour Group (which included two other ASRS-sponsored MPs from 1906). He now found himself heading a wave of discontent. In Newport, Tom Richards MP – and general secretary of the South Wales Miners Federation – warned that Labour would introduce a parliamentary bill in the next session to nationalise the railways, as Japan had recently done. Such a proposal met with the support of DJ Rees, the editor of Llais Llafur, who also had some advice for the railway workers:

> What is needed, then? To nationalise the railways; the country to own the fruits of its sons' labour ... But for as long as our railway men are so foolish as to send Tory and Liberal directors to represent them in St. Stephen's, and Richard Bell and his sort to plead for crumbs from Westminster's table of state, as to tip their hats obsequiously to neatly-dressed robbers and nestle under the wing of the same party as them, then so long will they take not one step towards liberation from their shackles; so long will they cry in vain for something better than a ten-hour day, and a pound a week in wages. There is but one path to salvation, namely to

cast aside the Richard Bells and the other Lib-Labs, and to take the path to victory and contentment under the splendid banner of Socialism. The Hardies and the Hyndmans must be chosen as leaders, and the Bells and Maddisons rejected for good. And there needs to be some weeding of the Independent Labour party as well, before it can become a suitable instrument for the indescribably important work that lies ahead of it, and which awaits its fulfilment. [13]

Alive to the fearful possibilities, Lloyd George wrote as President of the Board of Trade to the Prime Minister on October 19: 'It is too early to put the Conciliation Act [of 1896] into operation but there is a real danger of a strike being rushed owing to the ill-advised insolence of the directors – witness their dismissal of Union officials – unless something is done at once to get into contact with them'. [14] Lloyd George urged the government to ask Parliament to make arbitration compulsory in railway disputes, if the employers maintained their 'intransigence'; towards the end of the month, he met the directors himself on two occasions.

At a mass meeting in London's Albert Hall on November 3, Bell declared that the ballot had favoured militant action in pursuit of recognition and the All-Grades Programme: 76,925 members had signified their readiness to strike, with only 8,773 against. At the same time, Bell also revealed the results of a census (the 'Green Book') carried out by ASRS branch secretaries, which indicated that 39 per cent of railway workers received 20s a week or less; 92 per cent worked a ten-hour day or longer; and 56 per cent of employees received no special rate for overtime. [15]

The enthusiastic rally stung Lloyd George into a new round of frantic activity. He called the employers' spokesmen and union leaders together in the same building – but not, at the insistence of the employers, in the same room. After scurrying to-and-fro between the two committees in the Board of Trade offices that day, November 6, Lloyd George eventually secured agreement for an elaborate scheme of conciliation and arbitration (based on arrangements already operating in the coal and iron and steel industries). In truth, the scheme had been drawn up by Samuel Fay, general manager of the Great Central Railway company, and presented to Lloyd George by the six company chairmen there that morning. After adding some finishing touches to it with the aid of civil servants, the latter placed it before Bell and his ASRS colleagues in the afternoon, refusing to accept any amendments. Lloyd George informed them that the assent of the railway companies had been forthcoming only 'after much difficulty'. Bell's delegation were then given 20 minutes to accept it – otherwise the government would call their bluff. [16] The ASRS representatives opted for acceptance. The proposals were subsequently endorsed by the leaders of ASLEF and the General Railway Workers Union and 46 companies, having been dubbed 'Lloyd George's scheme' by an admiring press.

The 1907 settlement established several sectional boards in every company, each board to consider the wages and hours of the grades within its remit; should the workers' and company's representatives fail to agree, the matter would be referred to the company's central conciliation board and then – if necessary – to outside arbitration. Agreements and arbitration verdicts would be binding for at least 12 months, with the overall scheme to run for an 'experimental period' of at least seven years.

Yet, significantly, the companies had not conceded the principle of trade union recognition: the employees' representatives on the boards were to be elected by the appropriate sector of the workforce, not elected or appointed by the trades unions; and all such representatives, unionists or non-unionists, would have to be employees of the company concerned (and therefore open to victimisation). Thus the scheme drew no distinction between union members and non-unionists in any respect; only at the level of arbitration could a full-time union official play any part in the new set-up. Outside these arrangements, the companies were no more obliged to acknowledge the existence of unions than before.

These deficiencies perfectly reflected the priorities of Richard Bell. He had told George Askwith (an official in the Board of Trade's railways department) that finding a satisfactory method of dealing with demands arising from the All-Grades Programme was more important than winning union recognition as such – indeed, he would not press the latter if progress could be made on the former. [17] But, above all, it was Lloyd George who garnered the praise for settling the dispute; he received the plaudits of the press, of the railway companies, Richard Bell and the King, and was given the Freedom of the City of Cardiff for his efforts. The vice-president of the SWMF, William Brace, hailed the 'wonderful' plan. ASRS organising secretary Jimmy H Thomas called it 'an honourable settlement'. [18]

Llais Llafur editor DJ Rees, welcomed the avoidance of a confrontation in which the balance of forces lay with the state and the employers, took pride in the role played by Lloyd George, and claimed that the scheme strengthened trades unionism, interunion cooperation and the case for nationalisation. [19] Not that support for the new scheme was unanimous: while welcoming the industrial truce, leading ILPer and Aberavon MP Ramsay MacDonald called the conciliation and arbitration system 'a disaster' – thereupon earning a rebuke from Mabon the South Wales miners' president, who argued that the scheme would work and that non-recognition was no bar to success. [20] Thomas Lowth, secretary of the small but militant General Railway Workers Union, had his doubts: 'it does not look to me like a very satisfactory settlement', he remarked, although it was at least a step forward. [21]

Exiled in Geneva, Russian Bolshevik leader Lenin noted with approval the verdict of the left wing of Britain's labour movement:

Justice, the British Social-Democratic newspaper, in a leading article on November 16, commented as follows on Bell's agreement with the railway companies: 'We cannot but agree with the the almost universal trade union condemnation which has been pronounced upon this so-called treaty of peace ... it absolutely destroys the very reason of existence of the union ... This preposterous agreement ... cannot be binding on the men, and the latter will do well at once to repudiate it'. And in the next issue, that of November 23, [James] Burnett, in an article entitled 'Sold Again!', wrote the following about this agreement: 'Three weeks ago the ASRS was one of the most powerful trade unions in the country; today it is reduced to the level of a mere benefit society ... All these changes have taken place not because the railwaymen have fought and lost, but because their leaders have deliberately or stupidly sold them to the railway bosses ere the fight began' ...

The Labour Leader, organ of the moderate Independent Labour Party, which does not even want to call itself socialist, in its issue of November 15 published a letter from a trade unionist railwayman in which, replying to the praise lavished on Bell by the entire capitalist press (from the radical *Reynolds News* to the Conservative *Times*), he stated that the settlement made by Bell was the 'most contemptible one that has ever occurred in the history of Trade Unionism', and described Richard Bell as the 'Marshall Bazaine of the trade union movement'. In the same issue another railwayman demands that 'Mr Bell ... should be called upon to explain' the nefarious settlement by which 'the railwaymen ... are condemned to seven years' penal servitude'. And the editor of this moderate organ, in a leading article of the same issue, describes the settlement as 'the Sedan of the British Trade Union movement'. 'Never has such an opportunity presented itself for a national manifestation of the power of labour'. Among the workers there prevailed 'unprecedented enthusiasm' and a desire to fight. The article concludes with a scathing comparison between the dire needs of the workers and the triumph of 'Mr Lloyd George and Mr Bell hastening to prepare banquets'. [22]

Lenin was quoting these responses as part of his case against 'trade union neutrality', against methods which 'involve a blunting of the proletarian class struggle', against non-socialist trades unionism which 'puts in the forefront unity of the workers for the improvement of their conditions, and not unity for a struggle that could promote the cause of proletarian emnacipation'. In Lenin's view, Lloyd George was 'the Cabinet Minister who played the role of lackey to the capitalists'.

Nevertheless, although not without some grumbling, the majority of ASRS members accepted the settlement. The railway workers had no overriding desire to embarrass their officials who, after all, had already signed on the dotted line; they were prepared to give the new system a chance. Another factor was the the undoubted goodwill felt towards the administration headed by Campbell-Bannerman and, from the beginning of 1908, Herbert Asquith: the Liberal government was bringing forward measures to set up an industrial injury compensation scheme, to provide old-age pensions, to institute a maximum 8-hour day in the coal mines, to establish a statutory minimum wage in some notoriously low-paying industries, and to open labour exchanges for the unemployed.

In April 1909 as the new Chancellor of the Exchequer, Lloyd George unveiled his 'People's Budget'; he wanted to give money to the armed forces, pensioners and some of the unemployed – and intended to raise it from taxes and duties on landlowners, brewers and others of the rich. His fund-raising proposals were designed as an alternative to raising tariffs on imports, a reaffirmation of the principle of 'free trade' – and a trap into which the House of Lords obligingly walked when it rejected the budget out of hand. To the delight of progressives and socialists everywhere, the Liberal-dominated Commons and the Tory-infested Lords were on a collision course.

And it was during the run-up to the decisive confrontation that their Lordships dropped another legal bomb-shell on the ASRS and the whole labour movement.

Four days before Christmas, 1909, the five Law Lords upheld a complaint by Mr WV Osborne, an ASRS branch secretary, against his union's sponsorship of parliamentary candidates and a political party (in this case the Labour Party). The Lords ruled that no trades union had the right to spend its money on any form of political activity. In practice, this extraordinary judgement would – unless reversed by fresh legislation – deal a crippling blow to the fledgeling Labour Party. Paradoxically, given Osborne's Liberal affiliations, this affair drove Labour into an even closer alliance with the Liberals as the New Year general election approached; the left and centre united in an historic struggle to assert the supremacy of the House of Commons over the House of Lords.

By this time, too, the rumbles of discontent with the working of the 1907 scheme could be heard on the railways. Elections to the conciliation boards had taken place in 1908, with 93 per cent of workers voting for trade union candidates. Throughout the following year, agreements and arbitrations yielded modest advances in pay and hours: for instance, GWR employees received basic increases of between 6d and 2s a week, together with higher rates for overtime. But the terms of the arbitrators' award were – like so many of the decisions reached under the scheme – binding for the next four years. [23]   As other disadvantages and deficiencies became evident, so discontent within the ASRS reached such a pitch that Bell was forced to resign as the Society's general secretary, and to stand down as a sponsored MP; his post and his place in parliament were filled by another Welshman, Newport-born JH Thomas.

Thus the biggest railway union – whose membership had not actually risen since the 1907 settlement – faced the future under new leadership; the Liberal government, fortified by its election victory in January 1910, prepared for a show-down with the forces of inherited wealth and power. Beside the constitutional battles that lay ahead on Irish home rule, Welsh Disestablishment, votes for women and the power of the Lords to veto progress on any of them, Asquith, Lloyd George and Home Secretary Winston Churchill could expect war on the industrial front.

2. The Baptists' Jerusalem

The Llanelli branch of the Amalgamated Society of Railway Servants met on Sunday afternoon, October 27, 1907, on the eve of the threatened railway strike. Although only a quarter of the rail workers in the Llanelli area were in the union, theirs was a well-organised branch. A majority of the local members had voted in favour of the strike; now, with John Brace in the chair, they decided unanimously to ignore a circular from the Great Western Railway company threatening strikers with the sack, resolving instead to send it to Richard Bell with a recommendation that he return it to the company ... unanswered. [1]

Jimmy H Thomas, South Wales organiser for the ASRS, addressed a crowded meeting in the Athenaeum Hall on Sunday, November 3; he hoped that an honourable solution for all parties could be found. Thomas also took pride in the claim, supported by the press, that the railway men had not used intimidation as a bargaining weapon – unlike, he was sorry to say, some employers. The ASRS leaders would, he announced, meet Board of Trade president Lloyd George 'with a free and open hand to negotiate'. Thomas prayed that, even at this eleventh hour, a satisfactory settlement could be reached. A motion was moved to express satisfaction with the result of the ballot and to declare the men's determination to stand firm; according to the chairman of the meeting, Councillor William Roberts, only four people present opposed the resolution. [2] As we know, however, the crisis subsided in the following three days due to Lloyd George's efforts. His conciliation and arbitration scheme was accepted without great enthusiasm by the Llanelli railwaymen and their militant neighbours in the large Swansea branch.

Not that the dispute had been a major talking-point for the people of Llanelli. Tinplate was the main industry of the district – so much so, indeed, that Llanelli was the tinplate capital of Britain. Back in 1795, the town could muster a population of just six hundred. Then came the entrepreneurs to organise the mining of minerals – men such as Alexander Ruby, who settled in Ffwrnes and founded the ironworks nearby; he and others then exploited the local copper and coal reserves. The river Burry was bridged in 1805, and one of the first canals in Wales was opened in 1812 between Cydweli and Llanelli. Ruby established a corporation with £14,000 of capital to build a dock and 4-mile connecting railway on the edge of the town; when opened in 1833, with horses pulling the carriages, it was one of the first rail passenger services in Wales. By the end of the decade, the track linking Llanelli to Pontarddulais had been laid; within twenty years, Great Western had constructed the main line from Carmarthen to Swansea, running through the town. In 1875, a 13-mile railway from Llanelli up to Cross Hands was incorporated with £105,000 of capital in the name of John Wadell and Sons, local coalowners. At the end of the 19th century, on the rim of the anthracite basin, to the north-east of Llanelli, the last new coal mines in south Wales were opened.

By that time, however, the continuing prosperity of Llanelli and its hinterland was based firmly on tinplate production: since the founding of the Dafen works in 1887, the number of tinplate mills in the area had multiplied to more than 60. By 1911 there would be 107 of them. As a consequence of these developments, therefore, nearly half of Llanelli's workers were employed in the tinplate industry; three-quarters of the borough's population were directly or indirectly dependent upon it for their daily bread.

Thus was the wealth created which could keep the distinguished dignitaries of Llanelli in the manner to which they had become accustomed: families such as the Stepneys, with their grand mansion near the parish church in Bridge street. Established in Wales since the middle of the 16th century, their military lineage included a commander who had died while leading the Coldstream Guards at the Battle of Inkerman in 1864. Such petty aristocratic families prospered alongside the town's flourishing civic institutions. By the turn of the century, the burghers of Llanelli could boast of their new Public Library, the Athenaeum Building (with its Club and recreational facilities) and of the handsome Town Hall, with its clock tower, dome and balustrade in best neo-Georgian style, opened in its own gardens in the town centre in 1895.

Impressive chapels were raised, too, such as the Tabernacle (1873), All Saints (1874) and Capel Als, meeting-place of the celebrated David Rees. More than anyone else, he had been the political and cultural voice and conscience of Llanelli in the middle part of the 19th century; a radical rather than a revolutionary, Rees polemicised and campaigned against landlordism, liquor, industrial and trading monopolies, the 'truck' system of company shops, slavery in America and British imperialism in India. He preached in favour of Disestablishment, public health and æ'thrift'; he supported the cause of Rebecca and her 'Daughters' against the toll gates – while deploring their violent methods.

In the same way, Rees spoke up for the People's Charter despite its 'ungodly, unprincipled and foolish leaders'. Following the unsuccessful Chartist march on Newport in 1839, he wrote in his monthly magazine *Y Diwygiwr ('The Reformer')*:

Recent disgraceful, deplorable and tragic circumstances require us to finish our essay on Chartism rather differently than we had intended. We were going to offer some congratulatory remarks to our brethren of every rank, because we would never have imagined that the Welsh people, among whom we thought family principles, the teachings of the Sabbath, religious feelings and political knowledge were flourishing like so many ramparts, would have run to the same inhuman, irreligious and presumptious extremes as the unstable and fickle French mob, as the ignorant and ungodly rabble of Manchester and Birmingham. Nothing was more certain in our minds than that there was enough political knowledge, natural sense and religious feeling in the land of our birth to prevent any of its classes from colouring the earth with their blood, from being party to a rebellion so stupid, foolish and irrational, and from joining a campaign so hostile to civil order, so destructive of social happiness, of family comfort, of every feeling that adorns us as men and as Christians; but we have been disappointed – our country has marked itself with shame – our nation is in disgrace – it is likely that, of those who bring upon themselves the name of 'Rioters', tens have been killed and others wounded; gentle widows have tears on their cheeks because of the men who fell in the tumult, deprived infants lament fathers who have gone to an untimely grave, and there are now in Wales many Rachels who will not be comforted as they weep for their children. In Newport in Wales the smell of the deadly powder has not passed away, and the horrible desolation of civil war is there for all to see ... Well, why did they go to Newport, before the soldiers like sheep to the slaughter? It is evident that some were enticed by conceited and unprincipled orators, others were influenced by their friends, and for the most part they were compelled to go. One can be confident that this wretched occasion will stand as an effective warning to the common people, to test their mettle, to guard against being mesmerised and deceived by men who are eager to become something at the expense and through the service of others. [4]

In the view of David Rees, 'Mr Monopoly' (namely, the ruling class) was 'too strong to be defeated on this ground – war and riot are his dung-heap'. Here was the authentic voice of Nonconformist Llanelli, one which reverberated through the town for the rest of the 19th century – a bold and progressive voice, but also a constitutional one.

The spirit of confidence and optimism that pervaded the town is captured in a pamphlet by Arthur Mee (author of *The Children's Encyclopaedia*), published in 1889 under the title: '1990 – Or Llanelly a Hundred Years Hence!' Expressed in the vocabulary of the time, Mee forsees and describes phenomena that we know today as the television, video cassettes and the jumbo jet. He predicts the Disestablishment of the Anglican Church in Wales; nationalisation of the land; the replacement of unelected Boards by elected local authorities to run the schools and operate the Poor Law; the prohibition of beer (and consequently the near-elimination of crime and a decrease in the size of the police force); the formation of a world-wide system of peaceful arbitration in place of national armies and navies; people living longer; compulsory work for all, with abundant time and facilities for sport and leisure – although not for gambling; and no more industrial conflict between employers and workers.

Llanelli would be the capital city of Wales in 1990, according to Mee, with the nation governing itself within a federal Britain. The British parliament would be located in Birmingham, London having been destroyed by an earthquake in 1920 – the very year that old King Edward had accepted the post of inaugural President of the British Republic. Llanelli would be at the heart of the 'metropolis of Wales', the Glamorgan coalmines having been closed upon their exhaustion. The town itself would boast a clean atmosphere, tidy streets and pretty villas for well-dressed 'artisans' in place of slums and industrial chimneys. The inhabitants would be more numerous and better-fed, speaking the English of the civilised world. They would also speak Welsh, Mee informed his readers – 'not the half and half gibberish to which you were accustomed, but the pure language of the loftier bards'. An electric tramway would run through Llanelli's main thoroughfare, the old Mynydd Mawr railway having been abolished with the onset of electrification; churches and castles would have been preserved, statues raised to famous local dignitaries, and a further education college built. But some landmarks would have disappeared: the Athenaeum would have been dismantled by popular demand, for example, after the corpse had been found of a man lost in its maze of passages and staircases. That 'absurd relic' – the fountain erected in honour of the Prince of Wales – would have been removed to the local museum, along with the giant spike from the top of the Athenaeum tower.

Apart from a few idiosyncratic ideas, Arthur Mee's vision reflected the aspirations of Llanelli's middle classes and Nonconformist intelligentsia of the time. Their lives, with their civic institutions, majestic churches and well-appointed houses set in pleasant gardens, were markedly more comfortable than the lot of Llanelli's working-class population. While the railway workers were steeling themselves for a strike in October 1907, the town's 'high society' was excited by the arrival of a Royal Command, instructing the 230-strong Llanelli Choir to sing to King Edward and Kaiser Wilhelm at Windsor Castle on November 13 – in English, Welsh and German. Yes, it was a very different world for the masses, as described by a minister visiting the town in September 1907 for the conference of the Welsh Baptists' Union:

> The first things that struck me were the dirty roads, the unhealthy smoke, and the tram being drawn by a horse. A narrow tram being pulled by a skinny horse is a sight worth seeing. It is one of those things from a previous age, a relic worth preserving and placing in the National Museum of Wales when it is established, after Llanelli has grown out of the barbaric state that makes such things possible ... As for the smoke, of course this cannot be avoided, in so far as all the tinplate and steelworks etc. have been planted in the middle of the place, with houses built wholly chaotically around them. Such strange and unhealthy disorder. What caused such senseless arrangements to be made is remarkable to us today. It is a wonder that people's health is as good as it is, in such harmful surroundings. [5]

Although this correspondent rejoiced in the town's collection of impressive chapels, he expressed his deep sorrow at the number of public houses to be seen in Llanelli – 130 in all, by his account; one tavern for every 94 inhabitants. This was a poor advertisement for 'the Jerusalem of Baptists the world over', a town with more Baptist adherents than any other place on earth. In the chair at the conference of the Welsh Baptists' Union, and deputising for David Lloyd George, was W Llewelyn Williams, barrister, scholar, historian and the Liberal MP for Carmarthen Districts. In his opening address, he called for Disestablishment and – for the sake of consistency – the abolition of religious instruction in state schools. As three-quarters of Llanelli's population spoke Welsh, the MP urged them to make more use of the language when not in school or chapel, as part of the wider effort to promote cultural enlightenment among the common people of Wales. [6]

Williams had been re-elected to Parliament in 1906 with 3,902 votes from the electors of Carmarthen and Llanelli, as against 1,808 for his Tory opponent. His majority doubled in 1910 against a Liberal-Unionist candidate, and in the second general election later that year Williams was elected unopposed. To the north of Llanelli, in the coal and tinplate villages, the farms and the cottages, the people were – to an even greater degree – Welsh in language, Nonconformist in religion and Liberal in politics. Nobody had challenged Abel Thomas, a grey and characterless barrister, in the East Carmarthenshire constituency, in 1906; he retained his parliamentary seat with a majority of 5,000 over the Tory in January 1910. The working class of Llanelli and the surrounding district still aligned itself , for the most part, with the Liberal Party.

At the same time, an organised labour movement was in the process of consolidation. By the turn of the century, there were twenty or so trades unions in the town, many of which came together to form the Llanelli Trades and Labour Council in 1900. [7] Although the Trades Council affiliated to the Labour Representation Committee three years later, many union leaders and activists regarded the 'progressive' wing of the Liberal Party as the parliamentary guardian of their interests. Local MPs Abel Thomas, Llewelyn Williams and before him Alfred Davies were at pains to proclaim their pro-labour and radical sympathies; indeed, Williams' candidature in 1906 had actually been endorsed by the Llanelli Trades and Labour Council. Divisions within and between key trades unions had also hampered labour movement unity and the development of separate and distinct Labour politics, thereby helping to perpetuate the Liberal hegemony.

In the tinplate industry, especially, a gulf existed between the mill men and the tin-house workers – a gulf widened by the impact of the McKinley Tariff on tinplate imports into the USA (which favoured untinned plate). When the Tinplate Workers' Union of South Wales, Monmouthshire and Gloucestershire collapsed in 1899, some of the tin-house men turned to Wil Thorne's militant Gas Workers and General Labourers Union; many of the men in the tinplate mills, on the other hand, went off to the British Steel Smelters' Association under the more 'moderate' leadership of John Hodge. [8] As well as these divisions within the industry, tinplate workers earned considerably more than those in most other industries: skilled and semi-skilled men, for example, usually received between 45 and 65 shillings a week – twice the amount of a typical railway employee. For tinplate workers in south Wales, therefore, Free Trade in order to halt unemployment was the burning issue of the day, rather than wage increases. By campaigning for a reduction in US import tariffs, the Liberals retained the support of many tinplaters who were concerned that Labour candidates would split the 'progressive' vote – as Ben Tillett discovered when contesting Swansea in the General Election of January 1910.

There had been talk of a challenge to Abel Thomas back in 1907, when the Anthracite and Western Miners' Association met to organise a ballot, although no agreement could be reached on the choice of candidate. [9] Only the socialist minority in the local labour movement argued with any consistency for a political break with Liberalism. Yet the socialists were comparatively weak. Attempts to sustain a local branch of the Marxian Social Democratic Federation (SDF) in the 1890s had failed; a Llanelli branch of the ILP was established at the second attempt in 1906 – twelve years after Keir Hardie had first addressed a meeting in the town. But in the second general election of 1910, in December, the ILP mounted a challenge to Abel Thomas in the person of Dr JH Williams. With little trade union support, he received 1,176 votes (nearly 13 per cent of the poll), behind the Tory candidate's 2,315 and Abel Thomas with 5,825 votes.

However difficult it was proving to unite the working class in political matters, they came together in ever greater numbers to watch and play a novel sport. Despite denunciations of rugby from the pulpit, and Evan Roberts' crusade against it as a sin which excited the passions, the game was scaling new heights of popularity. This was particularly true in Llanelli, where the premier rugby club was winning sufficient glory to rank alongside Swansea, Cardiff and Newport. The 1909-10 season had also been a successful one for St Alban's RFC; the team came second in the Llanelli and District League, inspired by its captain John 'Jack' John. A young man of 20, employed at Morewood's tinplate mills, Jack John lived with his family in Railway Terrace. He was, according to a local rugby reporter, 'one of the most popular young men in the town'. [10] Another commentator on Llanelli's rugby scene remarked: 'Jack John, last season's skipper, seizes his opportunity in the twinkle of an eye, and always does his "whack". On the defence he is sound'. [11]

When St. Alban's RFC folded at the end of 1910, Jack transferred to the Oriental

Stars. Within weeks, the Stars were touring France over the Christmas, where they defeated national champions Bordeaux. Jack John, the talented centre, had already become a local hero; great things were expected of him on the Oriental Stars' tour of France scheduled for the autumn of 1911.

One hundred miles away in Redditch, Worcestershire, the Spiers family had earned a reputation of a different kind: all the men were soldiers. Harold Spiers had followed in the footsteps of his father and two older brothers when he enrolled in the Territorial Division of the 8th Battalion, Worcester Regiment. After serving his apprenticeship in the family's bicycle business, he enlisted as a professional soldier in the 1st Battalion of the Worcester Regiment in July 1909, at the age of twenty. [12] His father, Joseph, and the rest of the clan in Grave Street, Redditch, took considerable pride from the fact that young Harold had upheld the family tradition.

3. The Great Strike

Railway workers rapidly lost any faith they may have had in the conciliation scheme. Very often, disputes went all the way to arbitration where – especially in the wake of the 1908-9 recession – the arbitrator's awards were less than than generous to the employees. Worse, the agreements reached through conciliation were usually binding for at least four years.

The railway companies 'interpreted' the terms of awards in their own interests, resorting to all sorts of devices (such as regrading, rescheduling hours, delaying payments and taking on part-time labour) in order to frustrate the spirit – and sometimes the letter – of the award. This situation became so bad that, of all the industries covered by conciliation schemes, only in the railway industry did the Board of Trade judge it necessary to lay down procedures governing the interpretation of arbitration awards. In addition, the companies still refused to recognise trades unions as such: full-time officials were excluded from sectional and central conciliation boards, although they could represent their members at arbitration. Real wages in the industry fell in 1909 and 1910, with few victories won in the campaign for a shorter working week. Local disputes became commonplace.

In June 1910, the ASRS executive warned the Board of Trade of the rising tide of discontent; later that year, the union's AGM condemned the 1907 scheme in practice as 'inimical to the interests of the men'. [1] The Railway Nationalisation Society stepped up its propaganda, while the *Industrial Syndicalist* claimed that arbitrators who earned £52 10s a day were holding down the wages of rail workers earning less than £52 a year. [2] By the summer of 1911, food prices were 14% higher than they had been ten years previously, whereas railway wages on average had remained the same. [3]

But the Liberal government took little notice of this deepening disatisfaction, being preoccupied with the People's Budget and the growth of the German navy. Then, from the first day of August 1910, the coalowners, the state and its forces of law and order faced a challenge of extraordinary strength and ferocity. It was sparked by a lock-out at the Cambrian Combine's Ely pit at Penygraig in the Rhondda, imposed by one-time Liberal MP DA Thomas. The miners had demanded higher wages for working in 'abnormal places'. More miners came out in solidarity, so that by

November 1 all of the Cambrian's dozen or so pits in mid-Rhondda were on stop. The miners of south Wales and Britain extended financial aid to the strikers. Then the Powell-Duffryn company decided to charge its miners for the waste wood they had traditionally taken home for nothing: 20,000 colliers in the Cynon valley, Maesteg and Monmouthshire joined the 12,000 already out.

Following a clash between miners and police in Llwynypia on November 7, Glamorgan's chief constable Lionel Lindsay contacted various military garrisons for assistance. Upon learning of this, Home Secretary Winston Churchill stepped in to halt troops at Swindon. But then news arrived of more rioting, this time in Tonypandy, early in the morning of November 8; so at 1.30 p.m. that day Churchill informed Lindsay that help would be forthcoming – 100 mounted police and 200 foot constables were being sent from London, to be augmented by 200 cavalry of the 18th Hussars; infantry would also be put on standby. Major-General Nevil Macready was put in charge of military operations. A ferocious clash occurred between police and pickets near the Glamorgan colliery, Llwynypia, early in the evening of November 8, when a miner was battered to death; brushing aside the misgivings of the Secretary of State for War, RB Haldane, Churchill authorised Macready to meet the wishes of the civil authorities and send in the cavalry. As more police were also poured into the Rhondda that night, rioting broke out in Tonypandy.

Further battles took place later in November between police, troops and miners in Tonypandy, Penygraig and Aberaman in the Cynon valley. Over the winter, in effect, Pontypridd and the Rhondda valleys came under military occupation: the Lancashire Fusiliers, the Royal Munster Fusiliers, the West Riding Regiment and the Devonshire Regiment were all drafted in. From January 1911, after Macready had been recalled to the War Office in London, they were under the command of Major Freeth. The ASLEF executive launched a voluntary levy of 6d among its members to assist the strikers and their families.

Violence flared up again in the spring and summer in Clydach Vale, Blaenclydach and Penygraig. In June 1911, the Miners' Federation of Great Britain rejected the call for an all-Britain strike and terminated its financial support. On August 12, the South Wales Miners Federation decided the Cambrian dispute should end; the return to work was completed at the beginning of October, on the terms offered twelve months previously. But by then, too, their demands had developed into the call for a National Minimum Wage for all miners – a demand conceded by Act of Parliament in 1912 after an all-Britain strike.

Winston Churchill came under attack from all sides for his role in the Cambrian dispute. The coalowners criticised his initial reluctance to send in the soldiers; right-wing Tory and Liberal MPs would have preferred total reliance on troops rather than any major use of the police. Keir Hardie, on the other hand, launched three debates in the House of Commons and called for an inquiry into police actions; he also upheld the right to picket, and accused Churchill of carrying out a policy of 'Russification' in south Wales – acting like a Tsar presiding over his militarised empire. In reply, Churchill congratulated himself on his impartiality, praised the police for their courage and restraint and – to his credit – declined to join the London press in its villification of the Welsh as a people. He was, he declared in a Commons debate on February 7, 1911, glad that the police had stood as the brave, blue line between the army and the people:

> Law and order must be preserved, but I am confident that the House will agree with me that it is a great object of public policy to avoid a collision between soldiers and crowds of persons engaged in industrial disputes. All such collisions attended, as they must be, by loss of life and by the use of firearms, do great harm to the Army, which is a volunteer Army, and whose relation with the civil forces of the country must be carefully safeguarded, and they also cause feuds and resentments which last for a generation. For soldiers to fire on the people would be a catastrophe in our national life. Alone among the nations, or almost alone, we have avoided for a great many years that melancholy and unnatural experience. And it is well worth while, I venture to think, for the Minister who is responsible to run some risk of broken heads or broken windows, to incur and expense and an amount of inconvenience in the police arrangements, and to accept direct responsibility in order that the shedding of British blood by British soldiers may be averted, as, thank God, it has been successfully averted in South Wales. [4]

A number of Liberal MPs and newspapers echoed the calls from Hardie, Mabon and the SWMF for an investigation into well-documented allegations of police brutality. Churchill declined, firmly but politely, to initiate any such inquiry. Aberdare miners' leader CB Stanton called for a 'fighting brigade of miners' to use counter-violence against the police. [5]

The summer of 1911 proved to be hot and turbulent one. Before the end of the Cambrian war, the National Sailors and Firemen's Union struck for recognition by the employers, and for a living wage. The epicentre of the strike was Liverpool, where the well-organised dockers and other transport workers came out in solidarity; Tom Mann chaired the transport workers' strike committee there. He was by now the leading advocate in Britain of 'syndicalism' – revolutionary trade unionism to overthrow capitalism and put industry under workers' control; he had written vivid reports of the Cambrian dispute after touring south Wales in October 1910. Together with Ben Tillett, Mann had also played a leading role in setting up the National Transport Workers' Federation.

By July 19, 1911, Cardiff docks had come to a stand-still; on that day, too, the dockers of Newport marched out to the call of bugles. Rioting broke out in Cardiff the following day and continued sporadically for a few days more (with some incidents taking on an anti-Chinese character); Barry docks were paralysed from July 21. Other workers such as the tram-drivers and pit-prop men left work in support of the seafarers and dockers. In Cardiff, Glasgow, London, Liverpool, Hull and other cities, the Lord Mayor mediated between the shipping companies and the seafarers' union. But even when settlements were reached, the other unions stayed out on strike in pursuit of an 'all-round' settlement: recognition for all trades unions by the major employers. By the first week of August, all of London's transport workers had walked off the job, led by Ben Tillett. The railwaymen came under pressure not to transport materials for anti-union and strike-breaking companies; they also saw the victories that began to be won in ports and cities around Britain.

In some areas, the rail unions were already co-operating with strikers: in Cardiff, for example, Great Western employees had tipped off the strike committee about plans to import strike-breakers by rail. Starting with the Liverpool porters on August 5, railwaymen began coming out in the centres of transport militancy. Unofficial action spread through the north-west of England and down to London; by August 14, few trains were running in most English cities, or in Glasgow and Cardiff.

The situation in the industry was further inflamed by the publication of the railway companies' half-yearly financial reports, which showed that they were making record profits and handing out substantial dividends; on August 10, for example, the GWR raised the dividend rate on its ordinary stock from 4 per cent (already up from 3.5

per cent in 1910) to 4.5 per cent in the light of 'bouyant' profits – an increase which alone would have funded a 5 per cent pay increase of one shilling a week for most GWR employees. [6]

Tuesday, August 15

Under pressure to call a general strike on the railways, the four main rail unions met in Liverpool and resolved to give the companies 24 hours to decide whether they would meet union representatives immediately, to negotiate the basis of a settlement; if the directors refused, the unions would have 'no alternative' but to organise a stoppage. On the same day and in the same city as the ultimatum was issued, two protestors were shot dead by a military officer.

Wednesday, August 16

Upon receiving a copy of the railwaymen's statement, Board of Trade president Sidney Buxton invited the rail directors to talks in the morning. Two days previously, the companies had declared their readiness for a show-down. The meeting with Buxton strengthened their resolve. According to the directors afterwards: 'The Government having assured the railway companies that they will afford them ample protection to enable them to carry on their services, the railway companies are prepared, even in the event of a general railway strike, to give an effective though restricted service'. Sir Guy Granet, general manager of the Midland Railway company, added that the directors had no intention of meeting the unions: 'No direct request has been made for a conference; the implied request contained in the resolution at Liverpool will certainly be disregarded. This [ie. a strike] has not been sprung on us. We have been making arrangements for some time to cover such a situation'.

Granet also divulged further information to journalists about the assurances given to him and the other railway directors by Sidney Buxton: 'The Government at our conference today have undertaken to put at the service of the railway companies every available soldier in the country. In this dispute the Government and the railway companies are necessarily working together ... we have got to stand firm, and if the men wish it, there will be a fight to the finish'. [7]

In the House of Commons six days later, Winston Churchill had claimed to have received a letter from Sir Guy complaining that he had not used phrases such as 'every available soldier' and 'a fight to the finish' – he had been misquoted by the

Daily Mail. [8] But to return to the events of August 16, Lloyd George assured the Commons in the evening that:

> Nothing is further from the mind of the Government than to intervene in favour of the interests of any party to the dispute. It is essential, I think, that the Government should preserve an attitude of complete impartiality in matters of this kind ... We certainly do not mean to give any guarantees, to lend any countenance to the theory that we had undertaken, whatever happened, to back in advance any party to the controversy.

At the same time, the Chancellor declared that the government had a responsibility to protect life and property, including that of the railway companies. But he pointedly declined an invitation to endorse Home Secretary Churchill's earlier statement that the government also had a duty to ensure food distribution. [9] A few days before, the Press Association had reported that 'all Post Office telegraph lines' were 'blocked with hundreds of telegrams to soldiers recalling them to duty in connection with the strike'. [10] Troops had been mobilised as soon as the 24-hours ultimatum was issued by the unions.

Now on the Wednesday, Field Marshal Lord Kitchener, commander-in-chief of the armed forces, called at 10 Downing Street where the Cabinet was in session; it was denied that his visit was related to the imminent railway strike. The same day, the Army HQ at Aldershot published detailed plans for troop movements and railway operational duties. Almost all of the 58,000 members of the armed forces in Britain were mobilised, as Home Secretary Churchill despatched troops to localities without waiting for the civilian authorities to submit a requisition: they were in Cardiff by Wednesday evening, and over the next few days there would be garrisons in Newport, Llwynypia, Barry, Llanelli and Fishguard. Army regulations were suspended so that commanding officers in the field should enjoy similar powers of over-ride, including the right to order soldiers to open fire without the permission of a magistrate.

On secondment to the Home Office, General Nevil Macready controlled military and police operations under Churchill's authority. Macready would later recall of his work during the railway crisis: 'Nothing could have been more harmonious or easier than my relations with the railway magnates'. [11] Between them, Secretary of State for War Haldane and Home Secretary Churchill had, in effect and without a resolution in parliament, placed Britain under martial law.

Thursday, August 17
The trade union executives travelled down from Liverpool overnight, to meet Labour Party leader Ramsay MacDonald in London at 7 a.m. From there, the general secretaries went to the Board of Trade's offices in Whitehall, where Sidney Buxton presented them with a list of questions about their case. Rather like schoolboys, they were then told to write out the reasons for their dissatisfaction. A senior civil servant then took the answers across the road to Downing St. where the Prime Minister had been presiding over an emergency meeting of the Cabinet. Herbert Asquith then met the union leaders, reiterated the government's determination to keep the railways running at all cost, to protect the public and property, but offered them a royal commission to investigate the workings of the 1907 scheme.

While considering the offer, the trades unionists submitted a question to the Prime Minister: 'Has His Majesty's Government done anything, is it doing anything, will it do anything to bring the directors and the men together?' The authorised message came back: 'The reply is in the negative'. [12]

Believing that a commission would report neither speedily nor favourably, the union leaders went to see Asquith at 3 o'clock that afternoon to reject his 'inadequate' responses formally; they also told him that his government's threatening remarks were unacceptable, and that the railway unions were as entitled as any other workers to fair treatment. In view of all this, particularly the continuing refusal of the employers to meet them, they would not postpone the strike. Herbert Asquith's reaction was in tune with his whole approach to the union deputation that day, recorded by the Board of Trade's specialist in railway affairs, Lord Askwith; the Prime Minister told the men: 'Then your blood be on your own heads' – and left the meeting. [13]

Having been assured of the support of the Labour Party and of the TUC parliamentary committee, the union executives began despatching some 2,000 telegrams from 4.30 pm onwards: 'Your liberty is at stake. All railwaymen must strike at once. The loyalty of each means victory for all. [Signed] Williams, Fox, Lowth, Chorlton'.

The effect of the telegram was electrifying: throughout the Thursday evening, the men walked out in droves; their determination surprised employers, the press, politicians and even the unions themselves. Hundreds of messages poured back into the headquarters of the railway unions. In Newport, south Wales, ASLEF organiser Henry Parfitt relayed the strike news to 2,000 workers from the roof of municipal toilets, while the local ASRS branch reported: 'All grades coming out; great enthusiasm'. [14] Over the next 48 hours, 5,000 Dowlais miners and many other workers struck in solidarity.

  Meanwhile, in preparation for the gathering storm, Churchill had urged Chief Constables to recruit as special constables 'public-spirited citizens whose position enables them to serve without pay' – in other words, a middle-class militia to supplement the forces of the state against the working class. [15] Nine thousand volunteers came forward, two thousand of whom were subsequently enrolled.

Friday, August 18
The headlines in Saturday morning's *South Wales Daily News* capture the drama of the unfolding scenario:

SOUTH WALES TRADE PARALYSED

RAILWAY STRIKE POLICY UNIVERSAL

Troops Charge the Strikers at Fishguard

EXPRESS TRAINS HELD UP AT LLANELLY

Military Despatched from the Camp at Cardiff

  Although some trains succeeded in passing through Cardiff and Barry on Friday, by the evening all traffic had been halted; every line in the Rhondda was closed and Swansea was described as being 'completely isolated'. According to the same report, Monmouthshire's railway workers 'almost to a man were loyal to the strike leaders', with only one of the county's four lines even in partial operation. Friday also saw fierce clashes between police and strikers in Newport, Neath and the Swansea valley. A pamphlet published after the strike by the pro-Liberal *Cambria Daily Leader* summarised the position that day as follows:

  In South Wales the determination of the men found general support amongst the public, although the greatest inconvenience was suffered. The Midland Railway quite early abandoned the attempt to work their line from Swansea. The

L[ondon] and N[orth] Western were similarly circumstanced, and the Rhondda and Swansea Bay were equally impotent. The Great Western made a strenuous effort to get men to run the restricted service, but their endeavour was a failure, and early in the day they abandoned the attempt. Railway transit as the public were accustomed to know it had simply ceased to exist, and trade throughout the district was in a state of paralysis. Collieries stopped, works closed down, shipping was brought to a standstill. Practically everywhere men were in a state of enforced idleness, and concern for the food supplies of the country became acute. [16]

In a vain effort to induce workers to break this solidarity, the Taff Vale and other companies offered double-pay to employees who would work. Troops and police were deployed to guard strike-breakers and other items of railway company property, but to little or no avail in Wales, Scotland, northern England and other parts. Financial returns published a short while later indicated that the Barry, Taff Vale and Great Western companies lost virtually all their income for the duration of the strike.

Llwchwr Jones of Cardiff was inspired to compose these verses, published a few days later:

Y Streic

Mae cynwrf yn y gwersyll,
Mae'r gweithwyr ar eu traed,
A baner uwch eu pebyll,
Yn chwyfio arwydd gwaed.
Daeth dydd cyhoeddi rhyfel
Cydrhwng a Pen a'r Llaw;
A throwd ardaloedd tawel,
Yn fangre ofn a braw.

Mae'r dwylaw wedi bwrw
Eu offer gwaith i lawr;
A masnach fawr ei berw,
Sy'n hynod ddistaw nawr.

Y gweithiwr droes yn filwr,

Y cledd sydd yn ei law,

I daraw gwrthwynebwr,
Cyfiawnder caib a rhaw.

Nid dial sy'n ei galon,
Ond ymwybyddiaeth dyn;
Yn dwyn tystiolaeth ffyddlon
Mai mwy yw, na machine.
Cyfiawnder yw ei weddi,
Am ddiwrnod teg o waith;
A'i ddwylaw sy'n ategu
Ei gri a'g aml graith. [17]

The Strike

The camp seethed with excitement,
As one the workers stood,
Above the tents their banner
Flew red, the hue of blood.
Come the day war was proclaimed
Between hired Hands and Master;
So tranquil districts turned
To haunts of fear and terror.

Hands once so busy toiling,
Flung tools upon the floor;
And trade that once was booming
Would not prosper any more.
The worker since turned soldier,
A sword clenched in his fist
To strike at his oppressor –
For pick and shovel justice.

Not with vengeance does he act –
But consciousness of being;
Bearing witness to the fact
Man's more than a machine.
Justice is his plaintive cry
A fair day's work, his demand;
Behold, there to testify –
The scars upon his hand.

The Cabinet met frequently through the Thursday and Friday. As the strike became more solid, Churchill despaired of winning the battle, lamenting at one point: 'The men have beaten us. We cannot keep the trains running. There is nothing we can do. We are done!' [18]

There was another sign that Churchill was losing his grip on the situation: he had swallowed the absurd tale relayed to him by Sir Guy Granet that a German agent named Bebel – a waiter in a Glasgow railway station – had funded the strike from the beginning; Herr Bebel, reputedly an associate of the Irish transport workers' leader Jim Larkin, had supposedly distributed £5,000 to Tom Mann, Havelock Wilson of the seafarers' and firemen's union, and Emanuel Shinwell. Churchill repeated this nonsense around his social circles in London. [19]

Lloyd George argued in Cabinet that Churchill's methods were failing, and warned that the use of troops was bound to lead to violence. When the Chancellor asked for authority to mediate between the employers and the railway unions, Asquith immediately gave his seal of approval before retiring to the English countryside for a period of rest and relaxation. Lloyd George, meanwhile, met the union representatives on the Thursday evening and Friday to elaborate the government's proposal for a three-man commission of inquiry which would act with haste.

Saturday, August 19
After Lloyd George and Buxton had first discussed settlement terms with the railway directors, an historic meeting took place at 3 pm in the Board of Trade offices: present and in the same room were Sir Guy Granet and GH Claughton on behalf of the companies; six union representatives (including Jimmy Thomas); Lloyd George,

Buxton, Askwith and one other civil servant; and Ramsay MacDonald. But sometime during the negotiations, the trade unionists heard of a statement released to the press by Winston Churchill – and which enraged them almost enough to wreck the talks. Part of the Home Office bulletin issued that day declared: 'So far as present information goes, considerably more than two-thirds of the railway men are remaining at their posts. Numerous applications are being received by the railway companies for employment. The companies report that defections have not been in excess of expectations'. [20]

Churchill summarised the situation somewhat differently in a telegram sent to King George V on the same day, admitting that two-thirds of the railwaymen were on strike, reaching proportions of 75 per cent in south Wales and 90 per cent among the engine-drivers. [21] During the discussions at the Board of Trade, Lloyd George wrote the first part of a letter to his wife Margaret:

> *Yn nghanol* negotiations *pwysig* [In the middle of important negotiations]. Got Railway Managers to meet me so that is at any rate an achievement I never hoped for. Favourable so far. Employers behaving well. I got workmen's leaders here & addressed about 40 of them. Made favourable impression. First time I have seen them. Shall wire. Two men shot in a row at Llanelly. [22]

At 11 o'clock that evening, an agreement between all the parties was reached along the following lines:

● An immediate termination of the strike and a return to work forthwith;
● No victimisation or punishment of returning employees;
● The conciliation boards to meet as quickly as possible to discuss all matters in dispute within their remit; and
● Companies and unions to give every assistance to a Commission of Inquiry which would examine the workings of the 1907 scheme.

> Lloyd George's jubilation at having hammered out a settlement (very much with the help of MacDonald) was recorded by Secretary of State for War Richard Haldane: 'There I sat in the War Office, with a General in each room with his ear glued to the telephone receiving reports as to military arrangements. Suddenly

Lloyd George bursts into our room exclaiming: "A bottle of champagne! I've done it! Don't ask me how, but I've done it! The strike is settled!"' [23]

Later in the evening, Lloyd George completed the letter to Margaret: 'Hardest struggle of my life but I won. I cannot even now realise quite how. As someone said, 'It's a miracle' and really looks like it. The Railway Companies have agreed to something I thought quite impossible'.

His colleagues marvelled at this success, too; George Askwith and Labour Party leader Arthur Henderson put it down to Lloyd George's appeal to the 'patriotism' of the railway directors in the midst of an international crisis. [24] France had launched a military campaign to protect its capitalist investments in Morocco; Britain stayed silent despite the French violation of several international treaties, because the action also safeguarded British capital in Morocco – and because France in turn gave tacit approval to Britain's intervention in Egypt. The German Kaiser retaliated on July 1, 1911, by sending the gunboat 'Panther' to the Moroccan port of Agadir, demanding a Moroccan port to compensate for French expanionism. Britain and France regarded this 'leap of the panther' as an act of aggression. Lloyd George, hitherto regarded as a 'dove' in his attitude to Germany, delivered a bellicose address to City of London bankers at the Lord Mayor's mansion house on July 21. By the following month, he was in favour of war against Germany and attended the Committee of Imperial Defence to draw up Anglo-French plans for a military confrontation. In September, Lloyd George horrified the royal family at Balmoral with his view that an early show-down with Germany would be the best possible course of action. [25]

The crisis subsided the following month, after France ceded two strips of territory in the Congo to Germany. Speaking in the Commons in November that year, Keir Hardie insisted that 'protection of profits and dividends' had been the real motive for all the international agreements concluded between Britain and other countries about Morocco, Egypt and Persia (Iran) – not the liberties of other peoples, nor the honour of our own people. [26] A year and a half later, Hardie accused Lloyd George of having done a secret deal with Sir Guy Granet, chairman of the Midland Railway Company: the employers would allow the strike to be settled, thereby making British troops available to protect British investments threatened by the Agadir crisis, while the Government introduced a Railway Rates Bill to permit an increase in railway fares. [27]

Whatever the weight of international considerations in creating the mood for a settlement of the strike, domestic factors undoubtedly played a role, too. The Churchillian strategy of all-out confrontation gave way to Lloyd George's more conciliatory approach as it became evident that the rail unions were united and determined to an unexpected degree; the three-day strike was effective enough to reduce the week's passenger and freight receipts by up to 40 per cent for many companies operating outside south-east England. [28] Britain's exports were hit and the spectre of food shortages appeared; the value of railway company shares, which had begun to fall in the middle of July, slumped on August 14 and did not begin to recover until the end of that month; engineers and Welsh and Scottish coal miners were threatening solidarity action; and public opinion was so clearly in sympathy with the railway workers that even a hostile, anti-trade union press had to acknowledge it.

Now the main problem was to secure a full return to work on the part of the strikers. When Keir Hardie and Labour MP George Barnes addressed mass meetings in Merthyr Tydfil and Pontypridd on Sunday, August 20, they already knew the outlines of the settlement. They appealed to the men to have faith in their union leaders. But as Barnes himself confessed in the Commons two days later: 'If the men in that area had known the full text and character of the settlement that was effected on Saturday night ... no re-starting would have taken place'. That is why, again in his own words, 'We had, of course, to put the best face possible on the settlement'. [29]

By Monday, August 21, most of the railway employees were back at work. However, as they discovered that the agreement had not secured union recognition from their employers, they began to voice their disatisfaction. Thus, for example, after hearing a report from ASRS organiser for South Wales and the West of England, W. Carter, the Llanelli branch passed a resolution: 'That this meeting assembled at Llanelly reluctantly accepts the settlement arrived at as a temporary arrangement, and demands that nothing short of full recognition of the railwaymen's societies and an immediate substantial advance to every railwayman can be the minimum for acceptation. Failing this the Executive to give the call for a continuation of the strike at an early date'. [30]

In the face of such sentiments, the leaders of the rail unions attempted to defend their position through statements like this:

It is important to remember that the railway companies have agreed in writing to accept the findings of that Commission, even if it recommends 'recognition' of the unions. We have no hesitation in saying that in addition to having won official recognition in negotiating the present dispute, our evidence before the Commission will be such that justifies us in saying that before many weeks are over railway workers will have won a charter long enjoyed by every other class in the community. We would therefore urge you to loyally accept the agreement and demonstrate your confidence in the Executives and representatives of the four societies, who, by working together, have not only shown their power and taught our opponents a lesson, but by the loyalty which has been displayed have swept away the petty tyranny that has for years been the cause of so much unrest. [31]

Having gone along with this analysis for a few days, Hardie now began to have doubts. Writing in the *Merthyr Pioneer* at the end of the week, he criticised the timidity of the union leaders: 'Despite the military backing of the Government, the directors were on their knees. Had the four executives declined the invitation of the Board of Trade they would have won just the same, and probably more handsomely. I say it quite openly that I think they made a mistake in going near the Government at all. Their doing so weakened their position and enabled the Government to claim the credit of having settled the strike ...' [32]

Above all, it was Lloyd George who received the accolades for achieving an industrial armistice. King George V congatulated him on behalf of a grateful country for his energy and skill in 'averting a most disastrous calamity'. [33] The king also expressed his thanks by telegram to Home Secretary Churchill: 'Much regret unfortunate incident at Llanelly. Feel convinced that prompt action taken by you prevented loss of life in different parts of the country'. [34] The roles of Churchill and Lloyd George will be examined in more detail later, along with the attitudes of the monarchy. Before then, there is the 'unfortunate incident' in Llanelli to be considered.

4. *The Shooting*

L lanelli was a town on its way up at the turn of the century. Its population of 26,000 in 1900 had grown to 32,000 by 1911. Not surprisingly, one of the biggest problems facing the municipal authorities was a shortage of housing for the expanding workforce. In the spring and summer of 1911, a new tramway and Drill Hall had opened and work was completed on the town's electric street-lighting system. The local harbour was enjoying its busiest period ever.

Among the popular topics of conversation were the uncomfortably hot weather and the poor performance of the Llanelli Harmonic Society at the Carmarthen National Eisteddfod, where Professor Walford Davies had judged the choir to be 'badly flat' in its rendition of 'How lovely is thy dwelling place' by Brahms. [1] But preparations for a grand wedding in September were striking a happier note: Meriel, the daughter of Lady Stepney, would be marrying Sir Stafford Howard of Thornbury Castle.

Although more than half of Llanelli's railway workers belonged to a union, the area had been largely untouched by the kind of unofficial strikes that were breaking out elsewhere from the beginning of August. [2] Nevertheless, a particularly bitter struggle had recently taken place on Llanelli's doorstep: the miners of Trimsaran had been locked out nine months previously, having rejected the company's new price list for working a fresh vein. Riots had erupted in and around the village in January, as coalminers fought with the police. Throughout the summer, too, the ILP was holding rallies in Llanelli's Town Hall Square, presided over by Dan Griffiths. At a meeting on August 14, Councillor David Williams of Swansea warned that a strike would occur in the area in advance of any official statement from the leaders of the railway unions; he called for the formation of a truly patriotic Welsh party to replace the Liberals, one which would promote the interests of the people of Wales rather than the careers of its own members. [3]

Despite this, the local authorities felt sufficiently confident on the eve of the national railway strike to send 25 Llanelli policemen to Cardiff, on Wednesday August 9. This was in addition to the 15 local officers who were already serving in Tonypandy, their secondment caused by the Cambrian crisis. After all, why should trouble be expected in Llanelli, a place where political violence had been unknown since Liberal Party supporters had heaved a brick through the windows of the Conservative Club during the 1885 General Election campaign? The rate at which the political temperature was rising in and around the town went largely unnoticed; nor was it widely appreciated just how much Llanelli constituted a weak link in the railway line connecting London and Cardiff to Fishguard and Ireland. The local railway station stood at ground level, unlike the elevated sites at Swansea, Cardiff and Newport; roads crossed the line at either end of Llanelli station – making it especially vulnerable to attack and occupation.

Thursday, August 17

News was expected from London of the talks between the railway unions, the companies and the government. Would there be instant victory – or the start of an arduous struggle against ruthless employers?

One of the leaders of the Amalgamated Society in Llanelli, signalman Jack Bevan from Half-way, told the local paper: 'We are out for victory, and our forces are ready'. [4] Then came the fateful telegram at 5 o'clock.

'Strike! Strike! Strike!' was the cry heard across the town as railway workers proclaimed the instruction from their unions. Local officials met at once to establish a Strike Committee and to decide on tactics. People flocked to the station, some of them occupying the signal boxes. To the delight of the crowd, the signal-keeper in the western box took flight; firmer action had to be taken to dislodge the man in charge of the station's main box. A mail train reached the outskirts of the town at ten-past-nine that evening, but the crossing was blocked by one and a half thousand people, including young men who had already smashed all the windows of the nearby signal box. Dockers' Union organiser William Pugh appealed for peaceful protest, and the stone-throwing came to an end. Other unionists delivered fiery speeches to the crowd: 'Trade unionists of Llanelli, see to it that the gates shall not be opened. No trains shall pass these gates without passing over us first of all', declared Jack Bevan. The passengers alighted, leaving the driver and fireman aboard.

When the Cork Express arrived at half-past nine, Bevan again announced to the applauding throng: 'That train is not going to pass this way, except over my dead body'. But William Pugh also counselled caution: 'Respect the property of the company. You can win the fight without resort to rough measures. This will be your property before long, because nothing can stand in the way of nationalisation of the railways'.

For sure, neither Inspector Rogers, Sergeant Britten nor any of the other policemen could breach this human barricade when they proceeded to the crossing soon after 10 o'clock in the evening. Limited to guarding the two trains and the Cork Express passengers, they had no choice but to acknowledge the supremacy of the pickets – and to join in the singing and other entertainments that lasted through the night. The crowd even held a mock election.

Friday, August 18
Another mail train arrived from Cardiff at a quarter-to-eight in the morning. With the Cork Express still blocking the way, it could not enter the station. But on this latest train were 120 soldiers of the North Lancashire Regiment under the command of Captain Burrows. They had been despatched from Cardiff at the request of the Railways Protection Officer at Paddington. [5]

As they approached Llanelli station, the troops were welcomed by local JPs Thomas Jones and Joseph Williams; they then took control of the signal box and – ignoring attempts at fraternisation – opened the gates of the level-crossing. Only when soldiers attempted to remove people from the track did the crowd turn hostile. With a contingent of plate-layers in the front line, masses of protestors threw themselves at the police and the military, regaining possession of the crossing. Captain Burrows asked Thomas Jones to read the Riot Act, but the latter refused on the grounds that the violence was insufficient to justify such a step.

A meeting was hurriedly arranged between the magistrates, Captain Burrows, representatives from the strike committee and officials of the Great Western Railway company. Thomas Jones drew up terms for a truce, whereby the two trains that had arrived on Thursday evening would be permitted to pass through while the soldiers retreated to the station for fifteen minutes. Although the strike committee and Captain Burrows agreed with the plan, the railway company officials were not prepared to recognise the right of pickets to control the level-crossing for one second, let alone a quarter of an hour. [6] The crowd was becoming equally intransigent. Pleas from Jack Bevan, Thomas Jones and others for order and calm met with a frosty reception.

It is not clear how the situation then developed: according to Carmarthenshire's Chief Constable, W. Picton Philipps, two trains subsequently went through without incident. [7] Although he was in his office in Llandeilo at the time, parts of his report were based on the testimony of officers present at the eastern crossing and the passenger station. Other witnesses including journalists, however, insist that nothing passed through on the railway that day. In any event, it was evident that the strike committee was already losing its grip on the picket. When the Fishguard Express arrived shortly after 10 o'clock that morning, protestors mounted the footplate to argue with the driver and to address the multitude. After two hours, the driver was persuaded to leave his train and the engine's fire was extinguished. The same fate befell the next train to pull up behind the Express. Around midday, Thomas Jones and fellow-magistrate Frank Nevill sent a telegram to the Home Secretary: 'Troops unable to cope with mob. Desire augmentation of force by nightfall'. [8]

The Chief Constable now asked for the return of his officers from Cardiff and Tonypandy. Reinforcements came at 6 o'clock that evening: 100 soldiers of the Devonshire Regiment, 150 from the Worcestershire Regiment and 25 policemen from Cardiff. As the commander of miltary forces in the Llanelli area, Major Brownlow Stuart met Captain Burrows, Thomas Jones, Frank Nevill, the Chief Constable and leaders of the strike committee in the Copper Works School. Of chief concern was the plight of the passengers still stranded in railway carriages; the strike committee agreed to act. Its chairman, local ASLEF official Richard Squance, appealed to the pickets who by this time numbered about two thousand: 'There is sufficient military at hand to clear this crossing tonight. Is it worth shedding blood for the sake of preventing a few trains passing through? Don't allow the dignity of Llanelli to be dragged into the mire by having bloodshed without cause'. [9]

The entreaties were to no avail. At about 8 o'clock that evening, therefore, the authorities moved decisively to break the grip of the crowd. Fifty policemen marched to the crossing with a military escort. Although many of the protestors gave vent to their scorn, sang 'Sospan Fach' and attempted to stand their ground, the officers eventually succeeded in opening the gates. Some local men volunteered to drive the engines, thereby enabling the trains – including the Fishguard Express and the Irish Mail – to go through at last. The reaction was swift and furious. The army of pickets swelled to 5,000 as charge after charge was launched against the police. The crossing was regained after a bloody battle. Frank Nevill read the Riot Act of 1716: 'Our Sovereign Lord the King chargeth and commandeth all persons being assembled immediately to disperse themselves, and peaceably to depart to their habitations or to their lawful business, upon the pains contained in the Act made in the first year of

King George for preventing tumultuous and riotous assemblies. God Save the King'.

The proclamation had no effect. Chief Constable Philipps called upon Major Stuart to send a bigger contingent of troops to the crossing, and so the Worcestershire Regiment marched out with fixed bayonets. This was enough to cow the pickets who, by 9 pm had yielded the crossing and the gates to the authorities. From then until day-break the following morning, trains were able to pass freely through Llanelli assailed by little more than a shouted insult or a stone through the window. By two in the morning, silence reigned at the eastern crossing.

Saturday, August 19

Two trains were hit by rocks as they passed through Llanelli in the dawn light of Saturday morning. According to a reporter from the *Cambria Daily Leader:* 'A glance at the demeanour of the crowds then comparatively small, which were beginning to assemble at various points, sufficed to convince me that trouble of a very serious character was brewing'. [10]

From 9 o'clock onwards, the number of pickets grew rapidly. The town's magistrates met and arranged to accompany the soldiers throughout the day; they also decided to close all taverns in the vicinity of the railway station at 2 o'clock in the afternoon, with Llanelli's other public houses shutting at 9 pm. In the Copper Works School, the strike committee convened to discuss the crisis which confronted them now that the majority of protestors no longer recognised the committee's authority. Indeed, most of those picketing were not railwaymen at all, but workers from other industries keen to demonstrate their solidarity. As Colonel Freeth informed the Home Office in a telegram from his Cardiff HQ, at 1.15 pm: 'The pickets are half-hearted on the whole and the strikers at Llanelly are under control; the trouble there comes from the tinplaters not from the railwaymen who are trying to keep order'. [11]

Despite this, when Chief Constable Philipps visited the station and the eastern crossing at about 2 o'clock that afternoon, he did not find the attitude of the crowds to be particularly frightening. As he returned to the town, an engine pulling seven carriages full of passengers reached the crossing. After starting from Cardiff at half-past ten that morning, the train had come through a volley of stones on its way through Neath. It halted briefly at the eastern crossing, stopped for ten minutes in the station, and then a little after 2.30 pm recommenced its journey to Fishguard. In the meantime, hundreds of people had flocked to the western crossing in an attempt to block the train's progress out of Llanelli. The way was cleared by troops, who then returned to the station. But some protestors continued on foot alongside the train; the driver had to slow down as he saw the Old Castle crossing being obstructed in the distance. Here was the chance for five or six young men to leap onto the engine's footplate. The driver could not prevent them from disengaging the gear lever and putting out the fire, not least because he was – according to the Chief Constable and other witnesses – blind drunk.

The train now stood immobilised about 250 yards from the station, between the first western crossing and the Old Castle crossing. Facing the engine was the Union Bridge, a vantage point soon occupied by members of the strike committee as they raced there from the Copper Works School. By moving the train out of the station, it was later claimed, the authorities had broken an agreement with the committee. Aboard the engine, the driver cowered in a corner of the fuel tender, under a shower of coal and bleeding from the scalp; the fireman was thrown to the ground.

Eighty soldiers of the Worcestershire Regiment rushed to the scene from the station. One of the youths who had extinguished the fire turned towards them and, tearing his shirt to reveal his chest, shouted: 'I have done the thing; shoot me if you will, but don't shoot my innocent comrades'. Along with his comrades, he was pushed aside at the point of a bayonet. The train presented an easy target, enclosed by steep embankments at either side. Along the crest of the southern bank ran a lane behind Bryn Road; the northern bank was crowned by the back gardens of High Street's terraced cottages. Large numbers of protestors and spectators quickly gathered in the lane and gardens. The soldiers formed one rank on the southern side of the railway line, facing the lane behind Bryn Road where many women and children were amongst the crowds; two other ranks of troops looked up to the back gardens of High Street. They and the carriages then came under a hail of stones, slates and railings from both sides. Major Brownlow Stuart climbed the northern bank in order to reason with some of the protestors. Reaching the back-wall of number 4 High Street with a military escort, Stuart urged people to desist from throwing missiles and to go home peaceably. If they refused, he warned, then he would have no choice but to order his men to open fire. As the barrage died down a little, Major Stuart shook hands with some of the onlookers and made his way back to the railway line.

But the siege soon began again, heavier than before. A soldier was floored by a lump of coal, and was heard by Benjamin Hanbury to exclaim: 'We will have one of them now'. [12] Upon seeing the wound, someone at the back of number 6 High Street hurried inside to fetch a bandage and then, according to one newspaper reporter, stood on the wall and asked if the soldier had need of it. Stuart asked magistrate Henry Wilkins to recite the Riot Act. A trumpet heralded Wilkins' feeble effort. Few protestors, policemen or railway passengers heard the words; the impact was nil. Stuart now threatened to give the order to shoot unless the area was cleared in 60 seconds. This only added to popular amusement; nobody took the threat seriously. While Stuart counted to 60, a soldier's rifle went off by accident; the bullet whistled past Stuart's ear and flew harmlessly into the sky.

At this, one young man at the back of High Street exposed his chest and yelled mockingly: 'It's blank, boys!' According to one witness, the man's name was local rugby star John John. A few days afterwards, Stuart would recall having noticed 'one young man in particular who jumped up and bared his chest, and dared us to fire'. [13]

John John and a dozen or more other people had gathered around the garden wall at the back of number 6 High Street to watch the tumult below. They were only laughing and shouting, insisted some by-standers; they were pelting the soldiers with all their might, claimed others. John Francis, a 24-year old tinplater who lived in Glanmor Place, was sitting on the wall with his arms folded. By his side was Benjamin Hanbury from Railway Terrace, a labourer on the railways. John John stood nearby. In all probability, the three were friends. They had been following the train before jumping over the wall into the back of number 6 High Street. John John was wearing a red shirt. Leonard Worsell, a 19-year old labourer who lodged at the house, had interrupted his shave to go out and see what was happening; he wore neither vest nor shoes. Another lodger in the same digs, William Bailey, warned him: 'You had better come away or else you'll get shot'. These young men, lined up by the back wall of number 6, made 'excellent targets' in the opinion of a nearby witness.

As Major Stuart continued to count, John John turned to Ben Hanbury and remarked: 'Don't move, they won't shoot'. After the first deliberate shot was fired, Worsell yelled: 'It's all right, they've only got blank cartridges!'

Some fifteen seconds later, a bullet tore into the throat of John Francis and hurled him backwards into the garden. Everyone scattered, one of them crying 'That's a bastard shot!'

John John was the next to fall, collapsing by the wall with a bullet through his lung.

Ben Hanbury fled towards the garden shed: 'I saw the flash of a rifle, and I instinctively ran to cover, and as I ran a bullet glanced off my thumb and hit John John down. It was this bullet that killed John, who was standing right behind me'. [14] From the shed, Hanbury then saw Leonard Worsell lying nearby, bleeding profusely. Together with a friend he carried Worsell into the house, lifting his body onto a table in the middle room and placing it next to John John. John Francis lay on the floor.

Half a mile away, Dr John Lloyd Davies and his family were dining at Avenue Villa when they heard the shooting. Then a message came for 'Dr JL' and his 17-year old son Reginald – who was set to follow his father's vocation – to go at once to High Street. They travelled there in the local butcher's gig. When Reginald tried to enter number 6 carrying his father's black medical case, a Boer War veteran blocked the doorway and growled: 'No bloody press photographers here!' [15] Once inside, Reginald and his father found another doctor, Arthur Brookes, already at work. He had been in the neighbourhood when the violence erupted. John John was dead. Leonard Worsell had been killed by a bullet through his heart. The doctors could find nothing on the hands of the two men to suggest they had recently been throwing stones or any other kind of missile. The landlady of the house, Mrs Morris, was beside herself with grief; other women in the house were crying, some had fainted; men were cursing and shouting. PC John Morgan arrived at the premises – and ran for his life after being attacked.

During the firing, some travellers had jumped from the carriages and onto the railway line. They had not been targets for the protestors, and none was injured. One of them told the *Llanelly Mercury:* 'I am an old soldier myself, and I know what it means to handle a hostile crowd, but I do not hesitate to say that, as far as I could see, there was no need for shooting. There was mischief brewing, one could see, but it was mischief that could have been dealt with without the use of the rifle ... there is no doubt that someone has blundered, and, as generally happens in cases like this, innocent people are the victims'. [16]

Not surprisingly, soldiers saw things a little differently. One anonymous member of the Worcestershire Regiment was quoted in the same issue of the paper:

> The first shot – a single one – was fired in the air. The crowd took no notice of that, and simply jeered and called out, 'We don't mind your shots. You have only got blank cartridges'. The second shot was ordered to be given, and this time

several men fired. For a quarter of an hour before the fire commenced we stood quietly on the line, while people put our lives in danger. We were ankle deep in stones all the while. The crowd laughed and jeered at all warnings. They did not seem to realise that if our firing began it could be deadly. Four of our men were injured.

Soon after the rifle shots, the troops were withdrawn from the track and confined to the station. The attempt to clear the line had been a disastrous and bloody failure. Meanwhile, the engine driver had escaped to the New Dock police station, a hostile mob hot on his heels. Some pursuers declared their intention to drown him in the dock. It was rumoured that the driver had been plied with money and drink to take some wealthy passengers to Ireland for a business meeting. [17]

Later in the afternoon, a large rally took place near the railway station. On behalf of the strike committee, Jack Bevan implored the miners of Tumble and the Amman Valley not to come to Llanelli in the light of that afternoon's terrible events. [18] But in a meeting brimming with anger, another trade unionist declared: 'Men are born into the world to live, not to be slaughtered and shot at like dogs. Were it not for the importation of troops, Llanelli would be as peaceful as it has always been. We Llanelli men do not want soldiers to teach us how to behave. This afternoon there has been cold-blooded murder, and there will be a heavy reckoning'. [19]

Tidings of the slaughter in Llanelli reached the negotiations that night in London between the government, the unions and the railway companies. An agreement was hammered out – but by then the 'heavy reckoning' had already engulfed the tinplate town in south-west Wales.

5. A Heavy Reckoning

As news of the slaughter spread, gangs of young men and boys roamed the streets of Llanelli, seeking ways to strike back at the soldiers. Troops guarded the railway station and Station Road bridge near the eastern crossing. The crossings themselves were now in the hands of the crowd. No train would pass through Llanelli that evening, not least because some of the track had been torn up. Magistrates ordered the taverns to close at 9 p.m. Shop windows near the station were boarded up in anticipation of trouble.

Late in the afternoon, clashes occurred at the crossings between police, soldiers and protestors; every window pane in the station was smashed. When a train arrived at the eastern crossing at 5 o'clock, the driver found the gates bound shut with chains. As he reversed the engine for half a mile, pickets outpaced it and smashed the points to block the retreat. The crowd gleefully discovered that the train was carrying supplies for the Devonshire Regiment: the carriages were wrecked and looted, with young lads later seen parading around town in military head-dress and tunics. Rioters also ransacked the GWR goods station without challenge from the soldiers and police standing nearby.

Subsequently, Chief Constable W Picton Philipps claimed that the forces of law and order had not witnessed these attacks. According to his official report, the police had been fearless in the execution of their duties throughout the weekend – under the resolute leadership of their Chief Constable. [1] On the other hand, journalists and other eye-witnesses claimed that the police avoided confrontation with the crowds on numerous occasions.

Trucks of hay were burnt first, then the other waggons were raided and set alight. Avengers reduced the fateful train – stationary between the Bryn Road and High Street escarpments – to a skeleton. All carriages for a mile to Llandeilo Junction were destroyed as people enjoyed their booty of clothes, beer, whisky, cheese, meat and other foods. Not far from the goods station, they discovered the train that had brought the Worcestershire Regiment to Llanelli; it received special attention. That evening, hundreds of people flocked to the docks area where the goods station and 97 railway waggons were ablaze: 'The glare of the lights made a magnificent spectacle', reported one local journalist. [2]

The attacks on the railway company and army property were not random. At the same time, it should be noted that the looting and incendiarism was the work of a minority only, some of whom were motivated more by avarice than any nobler desire. A smaller minority still were railway workers. At eight o'clock in the evening, in Stepney street, the windows of the vegetable shop belonging to Mr DC Parry, former chairman of Carmarthenshire County Council, were shattered. Then, half an hour later, a contingent of men marched from the railway station to the grocery shop of Thomas Jones – the town's senior magistrate – in Market street. A block of concrete was hurled through the shop window as younger boys joined in the siege. Within minutes, they had smashed every one of the twelve panes of glass in the front of the three-storey building. The caution voiced by older members of the crowd that filled the street was brushed aside: 'If it had not been for Tom Jones', argued one of the assailants, 'those men would not have been killed at the station today. Bringing the military into the town has been the cause of all the trouble, and we are going to have revenge'. [3]

By the time Picton Philipps reached Market street with 40 police officers and 150 soldiers from the Worcesterhire Regiment, many of the protestors had progressed to Goring street and 'Brynmair', the mansion-house of Thomas Jones. He was not at home, having taken refuge in the house of a Councillor Simlett. Once again, Picton Philipps and his posse arrived after the outlaws had moved on ... this time to Hall street, where they attacked the ironmonger's shop run by magistrate Henry Wilkins. From there, the crowd returned to Thomas Jones' premises in Market street with the intention of razing it to the ground. By this time Picton Philipps was closing in on them, his men clearing Hall street before rushing up Market street and flaying everyone within reach of their batons. For an hour, the Chief Constable and his officers defended the grocer's stores against repeated onslaughts. Eventually, the police and troops retreated to the police station at the top of the street, although they had succeeded in seizing one of the ringleaders.

Throughout the turmoil, the arguments raged about the events of the afternoon: 'You know the gravity of the position when the Riot Act is read', declared one soldier; 'Yes', someone had replied, 'but what we say is that there was no occasion for the Riot Act to be read, and that if those men had not been fired upon at the station, none of us would be here. You shall see what the colliers can do!' [4] The mass of people could not be cowed by constabulary nor soldiery. According to one witness, Picton

Philipps and his men were treated like 'an army of schoolboys' as people laid waste to Thomas Jones' stores. A local newspaper correspondent described the scene: 'Biscuit tins were kicked about like footballs, large boxes of butter were carried away, and the account books, ledgers etc. of the firm were taken out and torn to pieces'. [5] While soldiers chatted with spectators, the furniture premises of William Davies and Sons were burnt down, with two horses perishing in the blaze. The rioters could not be dispersed until midnight, after a vigorous charge by the police and troops of the Royal Sussex Regiment.

There had been many other charges that night as the authorities tried to defend particular buildings. The fighting outside the Stepney Hotel was especially fierce: at least four policemen were injured (constables John Davies, Tudor, Thomas from Llandeilo and Sergeant Davies). Among those to experience the police batons was TG Anfield of James street, a solicitor's clerk who fell in the battle of Falcon Bridge.

At around 11 o'clock, the darkness was lit up by a stunning explosion in the vicinity of the railway station. There, in the sidings, stood waggons loaded with materiel such as gelatin, petroleum, carbide and gun powder. The likelihood is that boxes of this deadly freight were thrown onto a bonfire by some of the looters. Fifteen minutes later, another blast shook the area. Carnage ensued, with people crying for help or shouting 'out of the way!' as they ferried bodies to the hospital. The dead included William Harris, 48, of 25 Catherine Street, a labourer in the Copper Works and a native of Pembrokeshire; Alfred Morris, 23, of 6 Burry Street, the chauffeur to Lady Stepney, who lost both legs in hospital before expiring; and Ann Fisher, 30, of 2 Back-of-Stepney Place, a labourer's wife whose face had been half blown off in the explosion. A firefighter related his frightening experience:

> When the explosion occurred we were, as you can well understand, startled out of our wits. The rumour was that some people had used dynamite to blow everything up, but it turned out that a quantity of carbide, used in the manufacture of acetylene gas, had been exploded. All around the truck containing the deadly carbide were a number of people, some of whom were looters, and all had to bear the full force of the explosion. When we went near the truck afterwards, one of my mates saw something underneath. 'What is it?' I asked. With that he took hold of it, and then exclaimed, 'My God, it's a man'. So indeed, it proved. It was the blackened remains of man, but so badly burned that

identification was impossible, except by his clothes. [6]

The corpse was that of Joseph Plant, 31, a fireman from Trimsarn. Nine other people were injured in the blasts, some of them seriously. While these dramatic events were happening, the Docks police station – sanctuary for the hunted engine driver – came under sustained attack. On one occasion, five hundred people rushed the station, putting windows through and hammering on the main doors which had been locked in the nick of time by the wife of Inspector Nicholas.

Shortly after 10 o'clock, a batallion of the Royal Sussex Regiment under Colonel Montressor, on their way from Ireland to Port Talbot, disembarked at the Old Castle crossing. From there they marched to the passenger station, meeting 500 soldiers from the Royal Lincolnshire Regiment who had just arrived. At the behest of Picton Philipps, the troops then proceeded to the docks to relieve the police station. There, towards midnight, bloody fighting broke out as crowds converged on soldiers from the Worcestershire Regiment who had been guarding Station Road Bridge. The sight of a soldier who had fired his rifle in the afternoon provoked cries of 'Murderers!' and 'Assassins!' One railway worker shouted, 'It's going to be a life for a life'; someone else declared: 'We are not going to stand this butchering'. When the soldiers raised their weapons and pointed them at the protestors, one man held out his arms and exclaimed: 'Fire, you cowards! We're ready to meet you!' The insurgents were driven back by the batons and bayonets of police and soldiers.

The Worcestershire Regiment launched into the assembly in front of the station, scattering bystanders who had merely been watching the flames from the deadly explosions. One such spectator, Walter John the boxer from Austin Cottages, heard a trooper vow: 'I am going to do my duty'. Then the soldiers had moved off in the direction of the railway goods station, only to turn back and charge the crowd. According to Walter John's account:

> I was standing with my back towards the soldiers, when I felt a prick in the back from a bayonet. I quickly stepped on one side, when another soldier rushed at me, and plunged a bayonet into my hip, and I came away without telling anyone, so as not to enrage the crowd. I met a friend, and told him I had been stabbed with a bayonet in the hip and kidneys, and the blood by this time was running down my trousers quite fast. I was very exhausted, and was nearly overcome by

the loss of blood, and I had to be assisted to the house. [7]

A supervisor at the Old Lodge Tinplate Works, Richard Gethin of Brynmor Road, received a head wound; one of his friends told the press: 'They have stabbed an honest man. Mr Gethin could not run as fast as I. It was a race for life'. [8] Some of the most violent clashes took place around the eastern crossing. The ground floor of the Station Hotel had to be converted into a field hospital, with Dr John Davies and his son Reginald managing as best they could. Reginald Davies later recalled: 'I was put in charge of the only ambulance. It was horse-drawn and seemed to take an age to reach the hospital. We had on board a stretcher case and two other wounded, one man over 70 years of age with blood dripping on to the floor from a bayonet stab in the head'. [9]

More than likely, the unfortunate patient was Thomas Griffiths of 4 Globe Row. At least five people were taken to the town's hospital with bayonet injuries, including Ivor Thomas of Havelock Street, Thomas Thomas of Globe Row and Frank Francis, a youth from Crooked Row. Certainly, these were just some of many casualties that night. Perhaps it is significant that the soldiers did not discharge their rifles after the afternoon's events; according to press reports, they had been restrained by a Home Office instruction. How different the situation might have been had a group of young men succeeded in their attempt to break into the Volunteers Armoury in the Markets area that evening. The police and some two thousand troops finally quelled the disturbances in Llanelli and the docks area by two o'clock on the Sunday morning. The crowds were eventually pacified by news of the settlement from London, by the perpetual efforts of the civil and military authorities and – in some cases – by an excessive consumption of alcohol. The body of old Tom Traherne was discovered in People's Park the following morning – he had drunk enough to bring on a fatal heart attack.

On that Sunday, too, the Home Office issued this statement: 'Reports from South Wales this morning show that everything is perfectly quiet. Order has been restored at Llanelly, and the railwaymen are returning to work. The military officers report that the railwaymen were not themselves responsible for the rioting at Llanelly'. [10]

This was a widely held view in the town itself, reinforced by the absence of railway workers from those arrested and charged with rioting and looting. Moreover, the railmen themselves expressed it at their meeting in the Copper Works Girls' School on Sunday afternoon, where they welcomed the end of the strike and collected six pounds, two shillings and sixpence for bereaved families. [11]

At around the same time, the military began to vacate the town: 500 men of the Royal Sussex Regiment departed for Fishguard while the Devonshire and Worcestershire Regiments left for Cardiff, leaving soldiers from the Lancashire Regiment to guard the passenger and goods stations. Seven hundred troops were established at Burry Port for fear of further trouble. On Monday morning, the police began to search houses and gardens in and around Llanelli for stolen property. Now politicians and the press began a campaign of slander directed at the ordinary working class people of the district. Winston Churchill led the pack, telling MPs on August 22: 'The Llanelly rioters, left to themselves, with no intrusion of the police, and no assistance from the military for some hours, in a few streets in the town during the evening wrought in their drunken frenzy more havoc to life and limb, shed more blood, produced more serious injury among themselves, than all the 50,000 soldiers who have been employed on strike duty all over the country during the last few days'. [12]

'Syndicalism' was behind the rioting in Llanelli, according to the editor of the *Times*. [13] The author of a series of articles on 'The Psychology of the Welsh Riots' in the *Westminster Gazette* concluded that socialistic ideas about organising a 'General Strike' were to blame — especially when spread among as riotous a people as the Welsh. [14] So loud did the chorus of defamation become that David Lloyd George was driven to complain that 'part of the English Press has referred to us in Wales as only half civilised, if we are civilised at all'. What of the disturbances in Liverpool and Belfast? Although nobody deplored the outbreaks more than he, the Chancellor suggested that 'the best thing for these critics to do instead of making prejudiced racial comments would be to look at this in a spirit of sobriety'. [15]

Not that the Welsh press was any less condemnatory of those who had turned out in Llanelli on that Saturday evening. For example, in the view of *Tarian y Gweithiwr* ('The Worker's Shield' – a Liberal paper despite its title):

The main tinplaters' town of Wales, Llanelli, has made its mark during the railwaymen's strike, its inhabitants have brought the town into disgrace, and from now on it will not be known as a peaceful town, but as the abode of rioters, thieves and drunkards. It is deplorable that such a reputation has been brought about by a crowd of noisy layabouts and jobless hooligans. [16]

The editor of the *Llanelly Mercury* exhibited more restraint and discernment, being: 'exceedingly sorry that the fair name of Llanelly has been tarnished to such an extent that it will take generations to efface it. The hoologanism indulged in was unjustifiable, and the attacks made upon private property by a very small section of the community were, to say the least, disgraceful'. [17] The local paper strove to differentiate between rioters, on the one hand, and trades unionists on the other. A similar approach was adopted by *Y Tyst*, the weekly journal of the Independents published in Merthyr Tydfil; its editor blamed an under-class of anti-social and criminal elements:

> We do not hesitate to say that most of the damage, and all of the looting and burning, has been the work of a class of lazy and godless hooligans. The people of Llanelli and Liverpool should not as a whole be blamed for the carnage, except on the grounds that perhaps a large body of good and peaceful people should have taken firmer measures to halt the rule of anarchy in their midst. We certainly believe that a regiment of religious and respectable citizens would be much more effective and successful in keeping the peace that soldiers and policemen. It is not the strikers who do the damage, but 'rebels' and dregs who are always ready to take advantage of any opportunity to commit crime. [18]

According to the journal's Llanelli correspondent: 'Thousands of Llanelli's best people utterly condemn the irresponsible young boys, and many of the strangers who have recently come to town to work, for lowering the town's reputation, and here there is not a shadow of sympathy or support for the despicable destruction and foolish plunder that took place. One can only blame the dregs of the town for such things as these'. [19]

The *Llanelly and County Guardian* also indicted the 'nomadic labourers' and 'the flotsam and jetsam of the highways and byways of the country' who had come to construct local transport and sanitation systems. [20] The prestigious monthly magazine *Wales* went further; its editor J. Hugh Edwards, Liberal MP for Mid Glamorgan (Neath and its hinterland), claimed: 'We have made careful inquiries, and we find on investigation that the riotous ringleaders in every instance were not Welsh either in name or birth, but were exclusively drawn from those undesirable aliens who have come into Wales in the back-wash from the other portions of the United Kingdom'. [21]

How true are these assertions? Who were the rioters and looters in Llanelli? During August and September, 21 people appeared in court charged with theft or receiving stolen goods. Of the eight found guilty of looting the stores belonging to Thomas Jones, or handling stolen property therefrom, seven lodged in the poor, working-class area around the stores; six of these were labourers, and only two had previous convictions. [22] It was rumoured that every house in the vicinity was choc-a-bloc with booty. A dozen defendants were accused of stealing or receiving goods from GWR wagons; six of them came from the nearby village of Dafen. Most had taken small, ornamental objects of little value or practical use, yet all but two were sentenced to two months' gaol with hard labour. The nine people charged with riotous offences received more leniency, eight of them being fined one pound each.

The authorities clearly preferred to draw attention to the instances of 'dishonest', selfish and covetous behaviour than to anything more noble or selfless. David Thomas Howells, a tinplate worker from Port Eynon, was fined 25 shillings for being a 'ringleader' in the disturbances. If the police are to be believed, he was a man of superhuman powers. According to their testimony, he led charges against the police at 4.30 pm in the town, and at 10.45 pm near the station – while being blind drunk on both sets of occasions. When cross-examined about Howells' four head wounds and blood-stained hair, Superintendant Rodgers agreed that the injuries had been caused by police batons and added: 'He was struck and deserved all he got'. The defendant was found guilty of being drunk and disorderly and assaulting a police officer. [23]

Examination of court and casualty records shows that most of those who took part in the fighting were workers and they were Welsh; two-thirds of them had recognisably Welsh surnames, for instance. The documentary evidence does not support claims that non-Welsh unemployed or unemployable 'dregs' played any significant part in the conflict in Llanelli on that Saturday. The events themselves indicate that the violence of the mass was not committed at random by aimless or mindless gangs of thugs, but rather it was directed by local people against specific targets. Subsequently, under the Riot (Damages) Act of 1886, Thomas Jones was awarded £957 in compensation and Great Western Railways £2,713. The twelve compensation cases in Carmarthenshire won a total of £3,742, representing 12 per cent of all the money paid out under the Act in England and Wales for the twelve months to November 1911. [24] Although some of the defendants were applauded on their way into the Town Hall on Monday morning, there is little doubt that a sense of shame was also settling upon the town's population about some of Saturday night's events. Few people were prepared publicly to defend the rioting.

One of the exceptions was Keir Hardie; in response to Winston Churchill in the House of Commons, on August 22, Hardie pointed to the hypocrisy of the ruling class: 'It appears that at Llanelly there had been some looting from the railway station, and that some of the workmen's wives carried away clothing, and the Home Secretary looks upon that as a justification for the employment of troops. I wonder does he forget the situation that occurred at Pekin during the Boxer rising, when not only workmen's wives, but ladies of title, wives of foreign representatives and missionaries' wives, and other ladies of presumably good character looted the Palace to an extent that would shame the looting by wives of workmen, and carried off bundles of silk wrapped round their waists. I have not heard that any soldiers were sent to suppress that'. [25]

Of course, as a socialist and a Scot, as an 'extremist' who refused to join in the attack on working class people, Hardie was himself an ideal scape-goat in the eyes of the Welsh Liberal establishment. As the editor of *Tarian y Gweithiwr* remarked, he and his sort were primarily responsible for corrupting the pure-hearted Welsh:

> The Welsh are enthusiastic, and in a crowd their enthusiasm catches fire and blazes, even in the face of opposition. When a Welsh crowd is at its highest pitch, but is also on its own without the English and other foreigners to incite it, an emissary of peace would easily achieve calm, and the singing by some of a Welsh tune would be more effective still ... Oh! It is a pity that in the enthusiasms of the Welsh there is also infamy, due to idle, godless foreigners who have no respect for man. The Welshman is not like that, but there are some devilish multitudes around him who are, and they are leading him in his naievity to suicide. [26]

As we shall see, such attitudes were part of a wider and deeper antagonism between Keir Hardie and the labour movement on one side, and Lloyd George and Winston Churchill – and the interests of their respective classes – on the other.

6. *The Man with the Gun at His Side*

On Monday, August 21, Sergeant Evans discovered the exhausted body of a young soldier slumped by the wall of the Eagle Hotel, New Radnor in mid-Wales. Harold Spiers, aged 22, was a Private in 'G' company of the 1st Battalion of the Worcestershire Regiment. He wore the regulation khaki trousers, a shirt and heavy boots, and had been vomiting blood on the pavement.

Sergeant Evans took him to the police station and gave him food and drink. After a period of questioning, Spiers confessed: 'It's no use telling any more lies about it, I am in the Army'. He admitted that he was a deserter, recounting a remarkable story about his experiences on the previous Saturday. [1]

On that day, Spiers claimed in his voluntary statement, he had been serving with his regiment in Llanelli, defending the railway line against rioters. During the confrontation, he had been instructed by his commanding officer to shoot a man who was sitting on a back-garden wall, and who appeared to be one of the ringleaders. The officer had told Spiers: 'You see that man on the wall? – Shoot him'. When Spiers refused, he had been arrested and placed under military guard in a room at the railway station. Later, amid the confusion caused by the firing of the goods sheds, he had escaped to walk from Llanelli to New Radnor – a distance of nearly 90 miles – eating apples, nuts and blackberries on the way. Unable to go any farther, he had collapsed near the Eagle Hotel. He had thrown away his service cap on the journey. When Sergeant Evans searched the prisoner, he found an army licence with the inscription: 'No. 142, "G" Company, Worcester Regiment'.

Spiers appeared before the New Radnor police court on Tuesday morning, August 22, accused of deserting his regiment in Llanelli in the early hours of Sunday morning. Evans read the defendant's confession, before Spiers was remanded in custody pending further enquiries. On Thursday, August 24, the prisoner was brought before Richard Harding JP at a special police court, commanding officer Major Brownlow Stuart having been contacted. A military escort consisted of one soldier from the Worcester Regiment and one from the Welsh Regiment. After Segeant Evans had read out the defendant's statement once again, Harding pointed out that the bench required to know only that Spiers belonged to a particular regiment and that he had deserted; the reasons for his desertion had nothing to do with the court, and so Harding ruled that this part of the evidence – which happened to be the greater part – be deleted. Corporal Albert Ashley of the Worcestershire Regiment proved his authority to receive the prisoner, and the court ordered that Spiers be handed over to the military authorities at 2 pm; the magistrates also recommended that Sergeant Evans be rewarded for his excellent work.

According to press reports, Spiers was sticking to his account: he had refused to shoot somebody 'in cold blood'; if the man on the garden wall had thrown a brick or a bottle at him, he (Spiers) would have been willing to shoot him.

The prisoner was taken to Cardiff Barracks, where he appeared before Major Lloyd of the Royal Lancashire Regiment on Friday, August 25. Spiers was accused of 'desertion whilst in aid of the civil powers'; he insisted once more that he had refused an order to fire. The case was adjourned until his regiment returned from the Rhymney valley. The following day, Spiers appeared again before Major Lloyd, where he pleaded 'not guilty' to the desertion charge and reserved his defence. A statement was read out from Major Stuart, who was still in command at Rhymney. Spiers was then remanded for a district court-martial. Later that day, Lloyd heard a summary of the evidence which, after Spiers had declined to cross-examine witnesses, was forwarded to Colonel Freeth, officer in command of the south Wales area who would preside over the proceedings.

Already, though, the news of Spiers and his story had begun to spread far and wide. He was praised for his heroism. Llanelli's railwayworkers expressed their admiration for him, and called upon the Labour Party to campaign for his release. [2]   The Swansea branch of the ASRS urged Labour MPs to join the struggle. Representatives of the Cambrian colliers passed a resolution to thank and congratulate Spiers for his courageous stand. Penygraig ILP declared: 'We appreciate and record our admiration for Private Spiers for refusing to shoot when ordered at Llanelly, and in our opinion the courage displayed by him on that occasion deserves the highest praise that can be bestowed upon him, and we demand his immediate release'. [3] Aberavon MP Ramsay MacDonald promised to look into the case. *Justice*, the paper of the Social-Democratic Federation, opened a defence fund, and the left-wing *Clarion* carried this poem by Rose Sharland:

The Great Refusal of Harold Spiers – Hero

'Shoot straight, boys!' the officer shouted
'The ringleader, there is your man,
These strikers deserve to be routed,
Twas well till their trouble began;
Such rap and low poverty flaunted
Make mock of your Empire and pride',
- But one man with courage undaunted
Stood still with his gun at his side.

'You hear me?' roared he, 'Do your duty!
Protect England's wealth from their greed,
Her statesmen, her power and her beauty
Will praise you for serving her need;
So shoot for old England, your mother,
Deserters the world will deride'.
He answered 'I shoot not my brother',
And stood with his gun at his side.

O hero! true patriots gird you
The knight of an oncoming day;
The spirit of justice that stirred you
Shines bright through the terrible grey
When England, arisen, takes upon her
The ethics of love for her guide.
Your name shall be spoken with honour
– The man with the gun at his side. [4]

Spiers was being elevated to the status of working-class hero, to the embarrassment of the authorities. It may not have been entirely coincidental, therefore, that reports began to appear in the press that would deflate any such image.

The *South Wales Daily News,* for instance, carried this notice: 'We are officially requested to deny the statement made by Private Spiers on his arrest by the police after his desertion from the Worcester Regiment when on special duty at the Llanelly riots. The officers state:- 'Spiers was never ordered to fire by the officer in charge. It is extremely doubtful whether he was amongst the troops on the railway at all, and he was not under arrest at the time he deserted'. [5]

On the same day, the *Western Mail* identified the source of these reports: 'Major Brownlow Stuart, in command of the Worcestershire Regiment, informed our reporter during the inquest at Llanelly that there was no truth whatever in the sensational statements made by Private Spiers at Radnor. He was not in the party which fired on the rioters, and, therefore, he could not have disobeyed the order to shoot, nor was he put in the guardroom at Llanelly Station'.

Spiers claimed that he been instructed to shoot one of the apparent 'ringleaders' who was sitting on a back-garden wall – but had refused because the man was not throwing missiles. This could have been John John, whose antics as described by some witnesses are consistent with being an apparent ringleader, without direct participation in the bombardment (although some onlookers testified that objects had indeed been thrown from the vicinity of number 6 High Street).

At the inquest, Major Stuart told the foreman of the jury that he had not given orders to shoot any person in particular; according to his testimony: 'I directed the soldiers to fire at the men who were pelting stones'. Stuart also recalled in his evidence that 'one man in particular jumped up and bared his chest and dared us to fire'. [6] This behaviour was attributed by some bystanders to John John. How, it might be wondered, had Brownlow Stuart responded to this challenge? That Major Stuart ordered a party of soldiers to fire at rioters is not in dispute; nor is the fact that John John became one of the victims. But was Harold Spiers among the firing party – and did he refuse to shoot? Certainly, he claimed to have seen the same deadly dance by John John as other witnesses; if not in the firing party, at least initially, he could still have been present to see what happened; or the third possibility is that he was never on duty on the railway line at the time, and had either retailed an account to Sergeant Evans based on hearsay, or invented a fantastic story that coincided uncannily with a number of unlikely facts.

By the time Spiers appeared before a military tribunal at Parkhurst Barracks on Friday, September 22, the charge against him had been reduced to one of going 'absent without leave'. He pleaded guilty. The president of the proceedings, Major Howell Jones of the Royal Garrison Artillery, and two other officers heard evidence from a number of soldiers challenging Spiers' story.

Yet these witnesses also contradicted each other: according to a Sergeant Fisher, 'G' Company had been despatched from the railway station to the town centre on the Saturday night; when it returned to the station at 2 o'clock on Sunday morning, Spiers was still present. No he was not, claimed Sergeant Malone. Moreover, Private Ashbourne recounted how he had found a kit-bag, bayonet and musket balls belonging to 'Private No. 774' – Harold Spiers – in the guard's van on a nearby railway siding at 11 o'clock Saturday evening. Yet Spiers' army licence number was '142'. In short, there were considerable discrepancies concerning the time and circumstances of Spiers' disappearance. Nor was there any mention of whether or not Spiers had been placed under arrest that evening.

Stranger still was the testimony presented on behalf of the defendant by Llanelli solicitor Ivor Stanley Owen. From the outset, he asked the tribunal to discount all previous statements about the behaviour of his client, since the charge against Spiers referred only to his being 'absent without leave'. The question of Spiers' membership of the firing party was therefore irrelevant, Owen argued. On the Friday, Spiers had gone with his company to assist the civil authorities in accordance with the Riot Act; he and the other troops had endured rough treatment on top of their miserable food, receiving no comfort from any quarter. This had had a deleterious effect on the defendant's state of mind. Spiers had subsequently been in a party guarding a train in the sidings. Making it clear that he was acting in line with the defendant's instructions, Owen then concluded that the sight of two men being shot by soldiers, in addition to the other unhappy experiences, had finally driven Spiers to take leave of his senses: he had fled, without thinking of the serious consequences for himself.

Owen agreed that it was difficult to believe that the soldier had walked the hundred miles from Llanelli to New Radnor by Monday 'if he was with his Regiment on Saturday afternoon', especially without any trains running on the Sunday; perhaps Spiers had received a lift from friendly farmers, the solicitor speculated (as if he could not have relayed the truth from his client!). Until that time, Owen pointed out, the defendant's military record had been an unblemished one; he had also served a month in custody. [7]

Spiers declined the president's invitation for him to address the tribunal; on the following Monday, he was sentenced to 14 days military imprisonment. This was a light sentence indeed, particularly in comparison with the punishment he could have expected had the charge remained one of 'desertion whilst in aid of the civil power'.

Numerous questions arise from the army's treatment of Harold Spiers: why reduce the charge against him, for instance, and through that ensure a lighter penalty? Why did Spiers forsake his original account, revolving as it did around his alleged refusal to fire upon an innocent man? And then, having abandoned this version of events, why did he did not thoroughly renounce it and replace it with a full and unambiguous account of his movements? There are strong indications that some kind of deal was cut between Spiers and the authorities, to save the army from further damaging publicity concerning the shootings in Llanelli – and to save Spiers from a substantial prison sentence. Without doubt, the Liberal government was keen to avoid the creation of a working class 'martyr'; on August 29, Home Secretary Winston Churchill's under-secretary of state, Sir Edward Troup, had been instructed to write as follows to the War Office:

I am directed by the [Home] Secretary to say that he has noticed in the newspapers the case of a private soldier who is reported to have refused to fire at Llanelli on the occasion of the recent riot and who subsequently deserted. Mr Churchill does not know whether the newspaper accounts of this case are correct and what the special circumstances may be, but he desires me to say that in his opinion if the alleged incident actually took place, it would be contrary to the public interest to make the case a cause celebre by holding a sensational court martial, and thus investing it with an unnecessary and extremely undesirable importance. Mr Churchill hopes that the course will be adopted which will most effectively avoid any undesirable publicity. [8]

Even before sending this letter, Troup had discussed the matter with General Macready. [9] Then, on August 30, the reports appeared in the press intended to undermine Spiers' credibility and heroism. Subsequently, the military tribunal hearing indicated that an accommodation had been reached with the defendant, involving a lighter punishment in place of martyrdom. Certainly, the parents of Harold Spiers were relieved by the mild outcome; their son's legal defence had been arranged by the Llanelli Trades Council, and now his mother and father expressed their gratitude in a message to the *Llanelly Mercury*:

57 Marsden Road
Redditch
Worcestershire
October 2nd, 1911

Sir – Would you kindly put us a paragraph in your paper thanking the Llanelly people for their kindness towards our son? Private Spiers of the 1st Worcestershire Regiment, as you will remember, was brought up for refusing to fire at the time of the large strike. Neither of us was in a position to attend the trial, and he was left to the mercy of complete strangers to find a solicitor to fight for him. We are sure people that we had never heard of nor seen turned out to be the greatest and best of his friends. We shall never be able to return our thanks to the kind people of Llanelly. We hope you will put this in your paper, so that they may see that we have not forgotten their kindness. We are sure the gentlemen of our own town would never have taken such interest if he had been a stranger to them, as our son was to you. Hoping you will do your best to oblige.

Yours truly, his father and mother.
M. JOSEPH SPIERS [10]

After spending a fortnight in prison, Harold returned to his regiment in October. On December 4, he paid £18 for his decommission from the army. [11] Ten days later, John Hodge MP enquired about the fate of the soldier who had refused to fire in Llanelli; the under-secretary of state at the War Office, Colonel JEB Seely, replied: 'No soldier refused to shoot on the occasion in question'. Then Will Thorne asked whether Major Brownlow Stuart had been punished for ordering the soldiers to open fire; Seely insisted: 'That does not arise out of the question. I am asked what punishment was meted out to the soldier who refused to shoot, and I say there was no such soldier'.

Despite the official efforts to bury the case of Harold Spiers, it achieved prominence again within months. At the beginning of 1912, a railway worker named Crowley was arrested for publishing a leaflet under the heading: 'HALT! ATTENTION! Open Letter to British Soldiers', which included passages such as these:

YOU ARE WORKING MEN's SONS. When WE go on Strike to better our lot, which is the lot also of YOUR FATHERS, MOTHERS, BROTHERS, and SISTERS, YOU are called upon by your officers to MURDER US. DON'T DO IT! ... Property can be replaced! Human life, never. The Idle Rich Class, who own and order you about, own and order us about also. They and their friends own the land and means of life of Britain. YOU DON'T KICK. WE DON'T. When WE kick, they order YOU to MURDER us. When YOU kick, YOU get courtmartialed and cells. YOUR fight is OUR fight. Instead of fighting AGAINST each other, WE should be fighting with each other.

When *The Industrial Syndicalist* reprinted the leaflet, Tom Mann was arrested as the chair of the paper's publishing board, together with the manager and two printers. [12] They faced charges under the Incitement to Mutiny Act, which prompted Keir Hardie to attack Attorney-General Sir Rufus Isaacs in the House of Commons: 'The right hon. Gentleman has said that the soldier is never called upon to fire except in a riot. Surely that is to forget the most recent case, of which a good deal was made in this House, that is the Llanelly case, during the recent railway strike, when two men who were not participating in what happened and when there was no riot in any legal sense of the word, were shot dead ... Undoubtedly, in giving advice to the soldiers not to shoot their brethren who are on strike, we are trying to save them from the commission of murder. It is always murder, sometimes justified, and sometimes not'. [13]

Hardie raised the issue again, when the Commons debated the annual Army Bill on April 1 and April 10. In the second session, he went so far as to propose an amendment allowing soldiers to opt out of involvement in industrial disputes. Responding to Hardie's remarks about the use of troops in Llanelli and the Rhondda, Colonel Seely claimed: 'Not one single striker engaged in a trade dispute has been shot by the British Army since the South African war'. There was, therefore, no need for Hardie's conscience clause. When Labour MP George Lansbury referred to the shootings in Liverpool, Belfast and Llanelli, Seely uttered one word: 'Rioters!' [14] Josiah Wedgewood spoke in favour of the amendment, remarking that: 'Obviously a man who stated that he was not willing to be used in connection with trade disputes would be able to refuse to go to Llanelly, or to fire on the people'. The amendment was defeated by 168 votes to 23.

Tom Mann was sentenced to six months' imprisonment, but was released after seven weeks of militant campaigning by the labour movement. Addressing a mass rally in Trafalgar Square in August 1912, his comrade Ben Tillett called on workers to form an armed force of their own; other speakers urged soldiers to turn their weapons on their commanding officers. Although, in September, the annual Trades Union Congress rejected a motion to replace the standing army by a 'Citizens' Army', delegates nevertheless demanded a public inquiry into police and army 'excesses' in Liverpool and Llanelli.

What of Harold Spiers? He re-enlisted to fight in the Great War of 1914-18, after which he settled with his young bride in her native France, staying there until his death in the 1960s. His son, Desmond, survived him and in the 1980s was living in Harold Spiers' native town of Redditch, Worcestershire.

7. Killing No Murder?

Soon after the shooting, a local newspaper reporter had visited Leonard Worsell's lodgings at 6 High St., enquiring about his family's address in London. Worsell's brother wrote the information on a piece of paper: 'L. Worsell, 40 Parish Lane, Penge, S.E., "Murdered"'. [1]

On Sunday evening, August 20, the congregation of Zion Baptist church expressed their sympathy for the families of the dead and wounded. However ambivalent the feelings about Saturday night's events, a majority of the town's inhabitants regarded John John and Leonard Worsell as innocent victims of the afternoon's proceedings. This was also the view of Llewelyn Williams MP, voiced in October after a long spell of illness and quiet.

The local columnist in *Y Tyst* spoke for the whole town when he declared: 'Hardly anyone in Llanelli believes that things would have got anywhere near so bad had it not been for the arrival of the armed forces ... Doubtless there would have been agitation and revolt against allowing trains through the area, but the shooting of innocent men early in the afternoon caused the townspeople to lose control of themselves, their nostrils flaring – to toss order and reason to the wind, and to plunge themselves into riot'. [2]

The editor of the *South Wales Press* agreed that it had been a fatal error to summon troops to the town early on the Friday morning: 'At that time there was no justification for it. The arrival of the military was like a red rag to a bull to the crowd and for a time they failed to maintain their equilibrium. It was a gross mistake to order the troops to come here; it was a colossal blunder to ask that the Riot Act be read early on Friday morning. The crowd which had assembled in the vicinity of the railway crossing were peaceful and good humoured'. [3]   A contingent of police officers would have been sufficient, the paper argued: the Great Western Railway Co. had been at fault, because it was responsible for calling for the military.

Another Liberal newspaper, the *Llanelly Mercury*, was more equivocal: while praising the 'bravery', 'valour', 'real grievances' and 'sound principles' of the trades unionists, it also recognised the 'right' of the railway companies to appeal for military assistance in accordance with the written authority given to them on Thursday, the eve of the strike. Who could blame Great Western for protecting its property in

Llanelli as best it could? And yet, beneath this same editorial column, the *Llanelly Mercury* characterised the company's request for troops as unjustified, especially as the police and union officials could easily have coped with any emergency. [4]

In truth, the chief concern of the *Mercury* was to exonerate Thomas Jones (himself a shareholder in Great Western) and other local dignitaries of any guilt. Thus the paper branded as 'erroneous' the resolution adopted by mass meetings in the People's Park and Town Hall Square, organised by the ILP on the Sunday after the shooting:

> That this mass meeting of the people of Llanelly is unanimously of the opinion that the following magistrates and officers of the Petty Sessional Division of Llanelly (Car.) are directly responsible for the fatalities of August 19th, 1911:-
> R.H. Sampson, Esq., F. Nevill, Esq., Thomas Jones, Esq., Henry Wilkins, Esq., R.W. Evans, Esq., Joseph Williams, Esq., W.W. Brodie, Esq., (Magistrates' Clerk) Superintendant D. Rogers, and Chief Constable W. Picton Philipps,
> and further expresses its condemnation of their illegal conduct, and calls for an immediate inquiry into the whole matter on the part of the Home Office and the Government.
> S. JAMES, President.
> D. DAVIES, Hon. Sec.

Copies of this resolution were sent to the Prime Minister, the Home Secretary, Llewelyn Williams MP and the Labour Party headquarters. [5] The *Llanelly Mercury* had been perfectly accurate to identify Great Western – and not Thomas Jones – as having called for the troops initially. But the paper did not see fit to mention the telegram sent to the Home Office by Jones and Frank Nevill at mid-day on Friday, pleading for military reinforcements to be sent to Llanelli. Thomas Jones would never be forgiven for that, nor for welcoming the first detachment of soldiers to arrive earlier that day. A week after these events, hayricks on his farm at Llandafen were deliberately set alight.

The labour movement was in no doubt that the decision to deploy the army had been a disastrous one, bound to escalate the violence rather than reduce it. As the *Railway Review*, journal of the ASRS, put it:

Like a thief in the night, before even it was decided to issue orders for a national strike, soldiers were moved to various strategic points. They were posted at all the principal stations, took up their positions with bayonets fixed along the lines, on bridges, and in the vicinity of the principal depots ... The regrettable incidents of Llanelly will long live in the memory of all as a tragic result of this blundering. [6]

The Executive Council of the South Wales Miners Federation sent a resolution to the Home Secretary condemning the government for 'so readily' despatching the military to strike-bound districts; the miners expressed their sympathy for the relatives of those who had fallen victim to the 'unwarrantable action of the military forces in firing upon unarmed citizens', adding that 'none of those whose lives were taken had committed any crime warranting the passing of the death penalty upon them'. [7] As usual, Keir Hardie stood at the head of the protest movement. The day after the shooting, he told a large meeting in Trethomas Park, Merthyr Tydfil:

> The Prime Minister said that if there was to be a strike, the Government would have the railways kept open even if they had to shoot down everyone. Today in Liverpool and Llanelly there are mourning hearts for good men who have been shot down simply because they were fighting for better conditions of life ... In the name of the God we all worship, don't call it law and order to shoot down men who are only asking for their Union to be recognised. The duty of the Government is not to promise soldiers to back up directors, but to say that not a single constable or soldier shall be sent to their assistance until they recognise the men's Unions. The Liberal and Tory Parties protect the rich when labour and capital come into conflict. [8]

Hardie elaborated his standpoint in the *Merthyr Pioneer* on August 26:

> There never has been such unconstitutional action in our time as this calling out of the troops. Ministers have been impeached for less ... The Russification of the country by Churchill and his colleagues has already gone further than is safe. Organised labour can stop it, and expel from public life the men responsible for it. The Featherstone murders cost the Liberal Party dear. Let the workers be warned in time.

Hardie went after Home Secretary Churchill in the House of Commons on Tuesday,

August 22, in an acrimonious debate on the use of the military in industrial disputes. Even Ramsay MacDonald bordered on the intemperate, reminding Churchill that Britain with its civil liberties was not a medieval state, nor was it Russia or Germany. For his part, the Home Secretary denied that the government had sided with capital and the railway companies against labour and the railwaymen – rather it had sided with the public by protecting the network of food distribution. How could a government do otherwise? There had been serious disturbances in four or five places, less serious outbreaks in another twenty, six railway stations had come under siege, there had been nine attempts to destroy railway track, and twenty bullets had been fired by soldiers. He castigated the Llanelli rioters for the results of their 'drunken frenzy.'

Hardie could not accept this interpretation of events. The first response of Churchill and the government to any industrial dispute was to despatch troops to working class distrcits in order to intimidate people, instead of pressing both sides to meet. Each time the consequence of such a policy was to make the situation worse; in the latest case, the troops had been turned into servants of the railway company directors. When Hardie insisted: 'At Llanelly there was no riot of any serious consequence, there was no looting or burning of railway waggons until the soldiers shot two men dead. That was the beginning of the serious trouble at Llanelly', Churchill interjected: 'Quite inaccurate'.

Hardie continued with his analysis: 'The men who have been shot down have been murdered by the Government in the interests of the capitalist system. The intention was to help thc railway companies to suppress this rising among the men'. His speech was in opposition to the Prime Minister's motion to adjourn the House until the cnd of October; Hardie argued that this would place the running of the country in the hands of the Home Secretary and the generals.

In his brief proposing speech, Asquith had named the members of the Commission of Inquiry: Sir Thomas Ratcliffe Ratcliffe-Ellis, Secretary of the Great Britain Coal Owners Association; Charles Beale, a drirector of the Midland Bank and a prominent figure in the City of London; Arthur Henderson, Labour MP; John Burns, the ex-socialist who was now a specialist in labour affairs with the Board of Trade; and Sir David Harrel of the Board of Trade, in the chair. The commission and its appointed members received an unconditional welcome from MacDonald and George Barnes. It was a Liberal MP, Chiozza Money, who pointed out that neither the settlement nor the commission guaranteed anything for the railway workers – while the government was busily preparing a parliamentary measure to allow railway fares to rise, as profits and dividend payments increased without hindrance.

With Churchill so much on the defensive about his personal conduct, and Asquith's brief contribution concentrating on the future, the burden of justifying the government's all-round record fell to Lloyd George. He clashed fiercely and repeatedly with Hardie. Lloyd George denied that the Prime Minister had threatened to shoot strikers in order to keep the railway lines open, contrary to Hardie's allegations at Merthyr Tydfil. Hardie insisted that the press had misquoted him: he had stated that the Prime Minister had threatened to use the army to protect the railways, and that this had left an unfavourable impression on the union leaders; he – Hardie – had inferred from this that strikers would be shot if necessary. 'Traitor!' shouted Sir Charles Henry; Lloyd George remarked that 'if anything could be worse than the offence it is the explanation. I say without hesitation it is contemptible'.

Also in reply to Hardie, Lloyd George justified the deployment of troops in Llanelli on the Saturday afternoon: the crowd had blocked the line, torn up track, pelted soldiers and knocked one of them senseless, and assaulted an engine driver. Nor was it true, the Chancellor added, that the government had failed to exert pressure on the railway directors to meet the union leaders. Once again, Hardie cut in to recall Asquith's negative response to the unions on Thursday when they had asked whether the government would do anything to bring both sides together. Now Lloyd George and Asquith were trying to divert attention from that episode; Ramsay MacDonald reluctantly intervened to confirm Hardie's account. Lloyd George then trumpeted his own efforts at conciliation on the Friday and Saturday, the success of which had not been called into question. The bone of contention was the government's conduct at the beginning of the dispute – in particular the decision to mobilise the army to keep the trains running, while failing to show a similar urgency to compel the owners to negotiate with the union representatives. Still, the Chancellor did not yield an inch to Hardie, Will Thorne, George Lansbury and other critics, ending his combative speech on a confident note:

> We have maintained the law, and not merely the law that affects capital, not merely the law that affects life, not merely the law of individual liberty, but also the law of combination. We protected the rights of the men on strike just as much as we

protected the rights of the others. We were prepared to do our best to see that there should be no famine in this land. No Government could have done less.

Lloyd George revelled in his performance, writing in a note to his wife Margaret: 'Fierce labour attack on Winston. Just spoken – smashed Keir Hardie'. [9] Llanelli's railway workers were less impressed when they met at the Copper Works school five days later, declaring their support for Hardie's 'justified remarks' in his confrontation with the MP for Caernarfon Boroughs. [10]

On Tuesday afternoon, August 22, as the parliamentary debate was taking place, John John and Leonard Worsell were buried at Box Cemetery, Llanelli. The large funeral procession had set off from the railway station and included tinplate workers, local councillors, rugby players and railwaymen. South Wales and West of England ASRS organiser W. Carter represented Britain's railway workers. Many workplaces in the area came to a halt as a mark of respect. Friends and colleagues carried the coffins, which were adorned with flowers. At John John's graveside, the Rev. Hugh Jones of Bethel Chapel read from the Bible, and the Rev. J. Lewis, Caersalem, led the prayers. The anguish and tears were heart-rending; the hymn *'O Fryniau Jerusalem'* was sung. Wreathes and other floral tributes were laid by representatives of the St. Alban's and Oriental Stars rugby clubs and Morewood's Mills, and by family, friends and neighbours. Less than twenty yards away, Leonard Worsell's headstone read:

ERECTED BY THE
LLANELLY TRADES COUNCIL & LOCAL LABOUR PARTY
"WORKERS OF THE WORLD, UNITE!"

Because they could not afford the funeral expenses, the Worsell family had asked the War Office for assistance. Four pounds had been provided because, in the words of an internal War Office memorandum, they were 'respectable people but in very straitened circumstances'. [11]

The inquest on John John, Leonard Worsell and the four explosion victims opened at the Town Hall, Llanelli, on the same day as the funerals and the parliamentary debate. Colonel Freeth believed that it should have been postponed and relocated in Carmarthen because of the intensity of local emotions; Sir Edward Troup and General Macready disagreed, and the decision was left to local coroner JW Nicholas. [12]

Most of the evidence was heard on the second day of the adjourned proceedings, August 29. Major Brownlow Stuart recounted his version of events on the fateful Saturday, recalling 'one man, in particular, who jumped up and bared his chest, and dared us to fire'. His cross-examination by J Lewis Phillips, the solicitor representing John John's family, provided some of the most dramatic moments of the inquest:

PHILLIPS: The Riot Act was read to the people on the High Street side?
STUART: As far as I know.
PHILLIPS: Can you say why four men were shot in one place and the others allowed to go free?
STUART: It is rather outside my evidence. I directed the soldiers to fire at the men who were pelting stones.
PHILLIPS: Can you tell me why you took the risk of wiping out one whole family? All these men were in No. 6 garden.
STUART: I do not know where the men who were unfortunately killed were staying.
PHILLIPS: You did not tell some of the soldiers to to fire in one direction, and the others in another, and distribute their favours?
STUART: No.
PHILLIPS: It is part of the King's regulations that you should exercise care in shooting people?
STUART: Certainly.
PHILLIPS: Especially when you shoot your own countrymen. You are not supposed to be so careful in shooting foreigners?
STUART: (No reply)
PHILLIPS: You decline to answer?

At this point, in response to Lewis Morgan representing the War Office, the coroner adjudged the question to be unfair. The interrogation continued:

PHILLIPS: Were any of the passengers injured?
STUART: I do not think so.
PHILLIPS: These are the circumstances that justified you to fire?
STUART: The stones were thrown towards the troops and the engine ...

PHILLIPS: Did you shoot because they assaulted you?

STUART: Certainly.

PHILLIPS: These are the circumstances under which you say you gave orders to shoot?

STUART: (No reply)

PHILLIPS: I would like a note taken of that. [13]

According to the Major, his orders were not to allow the trains to be held up 'under any circumstances', and to use such force as may be necessary to enable them to proceed. He agreed with Lewis Phillips that he had failed in this objective on August 19, taking personal responsibility for what transpired. In his representations to the inquest, ASLEF organising secretary Henry Parfitt did not mince words. He told Brownlow Stuart that 'murder' had been committed and 'this misuse of the military is wholly responsible for all the looting and destruction, inlcuding loss of other lives, which took place at Llanelli afterwards'.

The coroner's brief summing up suggested on no less than five occasions that 'justifiable homicide' might be the most appropriate verdict in the cases of John John and Leonard Worsell. Nicholas bluntly told the jury: 'It is a sound proposition in law that if a riot is going on, the officer in charge is justified in killing'. Although the majority of witnesses testified that neither John, Worsell nor the others at 6 High Street had been throwing missiles, and Dr Arthur Brookes confirmed that nothing had been found in the hands of the deceased five minutes after the shooting, the coroner declared: 'It is quite immaterial whether these young men were actual rioters or not. As a matter of fact, they were among those who were in the direction from which the stones came'. [14]

After retiring for just over half an hour, and returning once to consult the coroner, the jury delivered its verdict: 'Justifiable Homicide'. Unusually, though, they added a rider: 'We think it would have been better if other means than giving an order to fire had been adopted by Major Stuart for the purpose of dispersing the crowd'.

In his pamphlet published soon afterwards, *Killing No Murder!*, Keir Hardie commented upon the jury's action: 'That rider destroys the verdict of justifiable homicide. If other means could have been tried before shooting was resorted to then the killing of the two men was felonious, and not justifiable, homicide – in other words murder ... The throwing of a few stones, even if one soldier be hit, does not justify the shooting of two respectable lookers-on, standing in their own backyard. It was the orders to protect blackleg labour which appeared to render that necessary'. [15]

The inquest jury had less difficulty reaching a decision on the other four fatalities: 'Accidental Death' caused by an explosion of detonators in a GWR truck.

The equivocal verdict in the case of John and Worsell could only have boosted the campaign for official compensation for their families. Many believed that their solicitors had won the argument at the inquest. On November 7, Liberal MP Frederick Kellaway – a close friend of Lloyd George – asked the Home Secretary in parliament whether such compensation would be forthcoming from the government. Reginald McKenna, who had exchanged his post of First Lord of the Admiralty with Churchill, replied: 'The answer is in the negative'. On the same day, Financial Secretary to the Treasury, McKinnon Wood, informed Kellaway that the Government had not asked the railway companies to contribute to the cost of deploying the Army; and on November 13, McKenna announced that the companies would be paid for transporting troops during the dispute.

Although the strike had ended, the political temperature did not subside. On Sunday, September 3, five thousand people marched through the streets of east London behind a banner with the inscription: 'In loving memory of and in sympathy with our comrades in Llanelly and Liverpool killed in the interest of Capitalism. Workers remember Trafalgar Square, 1877; Mitchelstown, 1877; Featherstone, 1893; Belfast, 1907; and now Llanelly, 1911'. The same banner led a procession through Llanelli on the following Sunday, behind the Kidwelly and Loughor brass bands. Thousands of workers wore black and white rosettes as they walked from the railway station to Town Hall Square, passing through the New Dock and Seaside districts. Money was collected for the families of John John and Leonard Worsell along the route. Presiding at the meeting in the square, Jack Bevan called for a change of leadership in the rail unions because the current leaders could not secure justice. The railwaymen had gone hungry, but the government had sent them 'lead' instead of bread; he warned that the workers would meet lead with lead if the bread was not forthcoming. Then, Richard Squence proposed the resolution: 'That this meeting of workers of Llanelli and district expresses its strongest disapproval and condemnation of the murderous action of the Government in placing State-maintained military at the disposal of private companies in the recent railway dispute, and demands a searching and immediate inquiry into the unfortunate shooting affray on Saturday, August 19th; further, that it expresses its deepest sympathy with the relatives of the two innocent victims, and calls upon all workers to combine politically, as well as industrially, as the only means of securing tolerable conditions now and justice and freedom ultimately'.

This was passed after speches from Dan Griffiths of the ILP, Thornhill from Swansea, and Ben Tillett. The dockers' leader delivered a fiery address. He deplored the 'silence' of the town's chapels in the face of murder, referring also to the 'Capitalist faith' and 'blood lust' of army officers. As in 1907, Tillett remarked, Lloyd George had played a key role as a government minister in mobilising troops against striking workers, turning the soldiers into a 'blackleg army'. The representatives of the capitalist class would use any means to obstruct the labour movement. But the courage of the people of Llanelli had taught the Liberals a lesson – and they would not dare commit an atrocity of this kind again. [16]

A series of meetings and rallies was held in Llanelli through the autumn, as the shockwaves continued to reverberate. At the beginning of September, the boys of Bigyn and Old Street schools refused to attend for several days, choosing instead to roam the streets; the chairman of the Llanelli Board of Education, Mr E Willis Jones, commented that it was 'a serious situation that some of the town's children are possessed by such a spirit of anarchy'. [17] Even the town's newspaper boys went on strike that month.

Later in September, indicating the local labour movement's blooming confidence, the Llanelli Trades and Labour Council launched a new weekly paper: the *South Wales Sentinel and Labour News*. Yet Llanelli had been a solidly Liberal town before the railway dispute.

Now the Liberals had to reassert their political leadership of the working class. Llewelyn Williams left his sick-bed to address a meeting in Greenfield School, on October 9, with characteristic skill and eloquence. He sympathised with the families of John John and Leonard Worsell – 'two poor youths ... who fell innocent victims of the disturbance'; he did not accept the inquest verdict and wanted an official inquiry into all the circumstances surrounding their deaths. While he supported workers' rights as much as anyone, he had also agreed with the Government's tactics during the recent crisis, and condemned the rioting without reservation. Most of all, he damned Keir Hardie. A week previously, Hardie had called for the creation of a

Citizens' Committee in Llanelli to campaign for justice, instead of a public inquiry which would merely whitewash the 'murder'. [18] Since then, Hardie had changed his mind in favour of a public inquiry, the local MP claimed: he was a 'trickster' who supported rioting. [19]

Defamatory remarks of this kind were repeated throughout the town's Liberal press: the *Llanelly Mercury* called Hardie 'an arch-trickster ... the Jeroboam of Scotland ... old hypocrite ... the old Scottish cormorant' and the suchlike – all in one brief editorial column. [20] A short while later, the local authority decided to levy a 'riot rate' of two pence in the pound on Llanelli's inhabitants, in order to pay the police for two days' overtime. With civic leaders deploring the impact of the disturbances on their efforts to secure a Royal Charter and borough status for the town, and traders and business people claiming that the district was missing out on new investment, the Liberals began to regain their local position of political hegemony.

The failure of the labour movement and its socialist wing to turn the dispute to longer-term advantage was demonstrated in January 1912. Following the appointment of Llewelyn Williams as Recorder of Swansea, his parliamentary seat was declared vacant according to custom and a by-election proclaimed. When Williams announced his intention to stand again, the Llanelli Trades and Labour Council, the Labour Party and the ILP decided to withdraw from the field. Only a small minority in the labour movement favoured putting forward an alternative candidate, as a protest against the despatch of troops to Llanelli during the railway dispute. They selected Frank Vivian to fight as an independent Socialist; he was an engineer in the gasworks, a 'representative of the working class' on Llanelli Urban District Council since 1899, and chairman of the council's Water Works Committee. He had also taken the chair of the Citizens' Committee established at the suggestion of Keir Hardie. The editor of the *South Wales Sentinel and Labour News*, Wilfred Thompson, would be Vivian's election agent – a responsibility he had shouldered for Victor Grayson in Colne Valley.

Vivian and his comrades strove to make the strike and the shootings an election issue, demanding a public inquiry and state compensation for the families; but Free Trade, the powers of the House of Lords, Disestablishment and national insurance dominated the campaign. Llewelyn Williams pointed to Vivian's lack of support from the local labour movement, and the *South Wales Daily News* referred to 'extreme

Socialists who are endeavouring to make capital out of the regrettable incidents connected with the railway strike riots last August'. [21] When Vivian's supporters raised these matters at a Liberal meeting in the Market Hall 'the large audience, mainly composed of workingmen, clearly demonstrated that they were not going to be led astray because a red herring of that kind had been dragged across the trail'. [22] A bee in the bonnet of few fanatics – that is how the strike, as a political issue, quickly came to be seen by the majority of local people. Vivian received 149 votes, compared with 2,555 for the Tory and 3,836 for Llewelyn Williams.

In August 1912, a parliamentary by-election took place in East Carmarthenshire after the death of Abel Thomas; here was an opportunity for the workers of Llanelli's industrial hinterland to demonstrate their anger about the events of last summer. Having claimed the right to nominate the Labour candidate, once again the miners could not agree on a name; once more, too, Dr JH Williams was left to carry the ILP banner with little support from the wider labour movement. The Liberals won a comfortable majority of the votes as the good doctor saw his percentage of the poll fall from 12.6 per cent at the General Election of December 1910 to 10.3 per cent in the by-election.

Not that the strike vanished completely as a political issue; rather it was taken over and sanitised by the local Liberal establishment. Every now and again, Llewelyn Williams would reiterate his call for a public inquiry, tabling a parliamentary question or writing to the Home Secretary. Had the local labour movement ploughed this same furrow instead of setting up its own Citizens' Committee, according to Williams, the government would have yielded. [23]

John John's aunt, Miss David, played a prominent role in the MP's lobbying of Sir Reginald McKenna. In August 1913, a deputation of local dignitaries including the Rev. Hugh Jones and solicitor J. Lewis Phillips, travelled to London to meet Liberal MPs; afterwards, Sir David Brynmor Jones (MP for Swansea District) and Sidney Robinson (Breconshire) went to ask McKenna for compensation for the two families. The Home Secretary replied that neither John nor Worsell had any dependants at the time of their deaths. In a letter to Llewelyn Williams, McKenna cited the verdict of the inquest that the army had not acted unlawfully in Llanelli, thereby absolving the Government of any responsibility to pay compensation. [24] On the same grounds, the Government rejected petitions in 1912 and 1913 from prominent local people including teachers, ministers of religion, solicitors, MPs and James Beynon of the

Citizens' Committee. [25]

In May 1914, the Pontypool and District Trades and Labour Council echoed the call for compensation, with JP and miners' agent James Winstone deploring the shooting; the railway workers of Llanelli repeated the demand in the following year, with no more success.

But to return to 1911 and the situation in the railway industry: on October 20 the Commission of Inquiry published its report. [26] By that time both the international crisis and the labour unrest in Britain had subsided. The report failed to advocate full recognition of the rail unions, contrary to their leaders' predictions, although it did concede the principle of recognition in an indirect and limited way. The chief recommendations to be welcomed by the workers were:

● The men's representatives on a Conciliation Board could elect whoever they wanted as their secretary, including a full-time union official rather than a full-time employee of the company concerned.

● Employers must reply to employees' petitions within 28 days instead of two months.

● Either side could summon a Conciliation Board meeting at 14 days notice.

● Agreements could not last for more than 12 months.

But two other recommendations made the ASRS, on balance, hostile to the report:

● The quorum of signatures required on a petition was raised to 25 per cent of employees in the relevant grade, up from 10 per cent.

● The Central Conciliation Board in each company would be abolished – leaving only the sectional Conciliation Boards, which employers had used to set one grade against another (but which also favoured ASLEF craft unionism).

This new conciliation scheme would run initially for a period of three years, after which either side could terminate it with 12 months' notice.

On November 2, the four rail union executives – backed by many branch resolutions and reports – decided to inform the Prime Minister that the commission's report was unacceptable unless amended: they wanted Asquith to arrange a round-table conference with the railway directors. The Prime Minister's staff informed the unions that the companies rejected any such meeting because the directors had agreed beforehand to abide by the commission's conclusions; now they would only accept minor modifications on a company-by-company basis, and only once the new scheme was operational. In response, the rail union executives decided to ballot their members on the commission's proposals, asking them about strike action and the need to formulate a programme of demands.

On November 22, 1911, Ramsay MacDonald moved a motion in the House of Commons: 'That this House regrets that the directors of the railway companies have refused to meet the representatives of the men, in order to discuss the Report of the Royal Commission appointed into the Railway Conciliation Agreement of 1907, declares such a refusal to be contrary to the public interest, and to have no justification, and asks the Government to bring both sides into conference without delay. [27]

Much of the ensuing debate centred on the claim made by the railway companies and Asquith that the unions, too, had agreed beforehand to be bound by the findings of the commission. A Board of Trade statement issued to the press on the night of the strike settlement had declared that both sides were willing to abide by future recommendations. Furthermore, it was now argued, the *Railway Review* (journal of the ASRS) had published a report, based on the Board of Trade's statement, referring to this pledge given by the railway unions. Thus Asquith accused the unions of bad faith, of trying to wriggle out of their commitments. MacDonald replied that the Board of Trade statement was merely 'a sort of unofficial addendum to the official statement'; it had been read out to tired men at the end of the negotiations, was unsigned and unnoticed. Another speaker in the debate, ASRS assistant secretary JH Thomas, hotly disputed the claim that the union negotiators had agreed to be bound. In the event, MacDonald's motion was diluted by an amendment from Lloyd George to delete all criticism of the employers, and to urge the Government to arrange a meeting between the companies and the unions 'to discuss the best mode of giving effect to the report of the Royal Commission'.

In a series of meetings between December 7 and 11, the unions won concessions on the petition quorum and notices of wage-cuts. But the abolition of the company-wide Central Conciliation Boards still stood. Even so, the union leaders signed the final agreement to introduce the new scheme. Many union members voiced their strong dissatisfaction with the deal, especially when JH Thomas refused to disclose the precise statistics of the ASRS branch ballot on the grounds that to do so would further embitter relations between the railway workers and their bosses. [28]

Swansea and 101 other ASRS branches demanded a Special General Meeting to discuss their union's position and the actions of its officials, although the call was rejected by the ASRS executive in March 1912. ASLEF branches in Llanelli and Swansea were among those censuring their union's executive.

Meanwhile, the unity created by the strike and the controversies surrounding it provided fresh impetus for organisational unification. The four main railway unions formed a joint committee which decided, in November 1911, to investigate the possibilities. ASLEF later withdrew, leaving the other three – the ASRS, the General Railway Workers Union and the United Pointsmen and Signalmen's Society – to ballot their members on merger. Out of this merger sprang the National Union of Railwaymen (NUR) in February 1913. In September that year, the new union's executive gave notice to terminate the existing scheme, but with a view to submitting a revised one. Across the industry, union membership spread rapidly: from a total of 180,000 in the three individual unions in 1912, to 268,000 in the NUR in 1913, to 273,000 the following year. Membership of ASLEF and the Railway Clerks Association rose to 62,000 by the end of 1914, turning almost every employee on the railways into a trades unionist. [29]

Taken together, the strikes of 1911 also inspired greater co-operation and unity between the major industrial unions in Britain, assisted by the great miners strike that began on March 1, 1912 and eventually won a Minimum Wages Act. In October 1913, the annual conference of the Miners Federation of Great Britain passed a South Wales motion to discuss an alliance with the NUR and the Transport Workers Federation. Thus the Triple Alliance was born on April 24, 1913, committing each union to solidarity action with each other – 'a powerful lever in the cause of working-class emancipation', according to the railway workers. [30] Events after the Great War would demonstrate that the vision was not shared by powerful elements in the leadership of that Triple Alliance.

8. History as Class Struggle

In the opening section of their *Manifesto of the Communist Party* in 1848, Karl Marx and Frederick Engels outlined the revolutionary role played in history by the 'bourgeoisie', the owners of capital. With a panoramic sweep, they described in dramatic style the revolutions in trade, commerce and industry, in science, knowledge and culture which had produced a new society from the ruins of feudalism. The burghers and other elements who comprised the bourgeoisie had subjected the countryside to the rule of the towns, created enormous cities, welded provinces into nations, and had centralised economic and political power into their own hands.

In what was also an international process, the extension of the railways had run alongside that of industry, capital and the power of the bourgeois class:

> The bourgeoisie, during its rule of scarce one hundred years, has created more massive and more colossal productive forces than have all preceding generations together. Subjection of Nature's forces to man, machinery, application of chemistry to industry and agriculture, steam-navigation, railways, electric telegraphs, clearing of whole continents for cultivation, canalisation of rivers, whole populations conjured out of the ground – what earlier century had even a presentiment that such productive forces slumbered in the lap of social labour. [1]

That social labour was performed by a new industrial working class, the 'proletariat', people without property whose only income came from selling their labour power to capitalists. But the worker can produce more wealth than he or she needs to consume in order to live (and to raise the next generation of labour power); according to Marx, the value produced by the worker's labour power is greater than the value of his or her wages. This 'surplus value' is usually realised by the owner of the means of production (the plant, machinery, raw materials etc.) when the commodities produced by that labour power are sold; it is the source of capitalist profit.

Here was the essence of what the *Manifesto* identified as a system of 'naked, shameless, direct, brutal exploitation'. Labour discipline ensured the maximum extraction of this surplus value:

> Modern industry has converted the little workshop of the patriarchal master into the great factory of the industrial capitalist. Masses of labourers, crowded into the factory, are organised like soldiers. As privates of the industrial army they are placed under the command of a perfect hierarchy of officers and sergeants. Not only are they slaves of the bourgeois class, and of the bourgeois State; they are daily and hourly enslaved by the machine, by the overlooker, and, above all, by the individual bourgeois manufacturer himself. The more openly this despotism proclaims gain to be its end and aim, the more petty, the more hateful and more embittering it is. [2]

The need for the capitalist to extract surplus value and turn it into profit, to turn more profit into capital in order to compete against other capitalists, created the objective basis for class conflict. Because the working class would increasingly organise, industrially and politically, against their own exploitation and to keep more of the value they produced, class struggle was intrinsic to capitalism. By the end of the 19th century, capitalism had entered another phase of development, passing from free competition to monopoly. Giant companies had come to dominate the different branches of industry and commerce, often working in cartels to fix markets, prices and profits. Monopoly capitalism extended across vast tracts of the globe, dominating countries and even whole continents economically and politically. The imperialist countries had carved up much of the world between themselves, fighting wars against subject peoples and against each other for the control of markets and territories. Britain's industrial supremacy was being challenged by Germany, France and – to a lesser extent – the United States. The bourgeoisie of these imperialist countries no longer played a progressive role in history, no longer fought for liberty and democracy against feudal reaction: they had themselves turned into reactionaries, suppressing the labour movement at home and national liberation movements in the colonies.

By this time, too, the railways had become the main terrestrial arteries of imperialism. In the two decades from 1890, their mileage doubled in the colonial territories, facilitating plunder, trade and the transportation of troops. Lenin assessed their significance in a preface to the French and German editions of his book

Imperialism – the Highest Stage of Capitalism:

> Railways are a summation of the basic capitalist industries, coal, iron and steel; a summation and the most striking index of the development of world trade and bourgeois-democratic civilisation. How the railways are linked up with large-scale industry, with monopolies, syndicates, cartels, trusts, banks and the financial oligarchy is shown in the preceding chapters of the book. The uneven distribution of the railways – their uneven development – sums up, as it were, modern monopolist capitalism on a world-wide scale. And this summary proves that imperialist wars are absolutely inevitable under *such* an economic system, *as long as* private property in the means of production exists. The building of railways seems to be a simple, natural, democratic, cultural and civilising enterprise; that is what it is in the opinion of the bourgeois professors who are paid to depict capitalist slavery in bright colours, and in the opinion of petty-bourgeois philistines. But as a matter of fact the capitalist threads, which in thousands of different intercrossings bind these enterprises with private property in the means of production in general, have converted this railway construction into an instrument for oppressing a *thousand million* people (in the colonies and semi-colonies), that is, more than half the population of the globe that inhabits the dependent countries, as well as the wage-slaves of capital in the 'civilised' countries. [3]

Herein lies an explanation for the hard-faced attitude of the railway directors, many of whom were investors in this and other industries around the world. They were conscious, indeed proud, of the place of the railways in Britain, the empire and beyond; these iron roads were, in a sense, the new industrial civilisation in microcosm, likewise to be maintained by ruthless order and discipline. For most of the rail magnates, therefore, trades unionism in the industrial army was akin to mutiny in the military one – something to be crushed without compromise. This view, applied across the economy, was shared by most Tories and many Liberals within the capitalist class.

For other Liberals, however, the enemy was not trades unionism as such, but socialism. They believed that Britain's employers and politicians should accept the need to bargain with labour, conceding improvements and reforms where possible, drawing trade union leaders into civic and political life. This would reduce the possibility of the working class turning to revolutionary ideas and actions. With more and more working men achieving the vote from 1867 onwards, it made sense to project the Liberal Party as representing the supposedly common interests of both 'moderate' workers and 'enlightened' employers. Class warfare was not inevitable, according to this approach, despite the efforts of 'hot-heads' and extremists to demonstrate the contrary.

David Lloyd George was a leading advocate of this 'progressive' Liberalism. In the first decade of the 20th century, he rose to become the leader of 'left-wing' Liberalism on the British stage, drawing upon the peculiarities of Welsh society to lend force to his views and values. Wales had not generated a powerful native capitalist class of its own, one of thrusting traders, entrepreneurs and bankers of the kind described by Marx and Engels – a new ruling class that would require a state apparatus of its own within Wales. By the time the Welsh coalowners had emerged, they were part of a British capitalist class whose interests were well served by the British state. Moreover, the British empire and its navy had been vital to the prosperity of the south Wales coal industry.

It was, rather, the class of small property owners – farmers, smallholders, lawyers, artisans, shopkeepers, clerics and academics – who came to exercise cultural, social and political leadership in late Victorian Wales. Historically, this 'petty bourgeoisie' had its own objectives as a class: to secure full freedom and equality for Nonconformism (and liberation from the thrall of the Anglican church); to establish an education system that would enable Welsh children to participate in the privileges of state and empire; to break the grip of the Tory and Anglican landowners on rural society; to provide moral, cultural and political leadership to a reinvigorated – and reinvented – Welsh nation, involving the creation of its own national institutions; and to win a respected place for Wales and its new leaders in the administration of Britain and the British empire. Most of these aims were accomplished in the final quarter of the 19th century, before the Welsh Liberal petty bourgeoisie crowned its political supremacy with the stunning triumph of 1906.

Nothing and nobody came to embody the aspirations of this class more clearly than the career of Lloyd George. Indeed, until the investiture of young Edward as Prince of Wales in 1911, Lloyd George was the unofficial 'prince of Wales'. His portrait adorned every middle-class journal in the country, his shoulders draped in an ermine-lined gown, accompanied as often as not by a verse or two in praise of the 'people's prince'. But as a government minister, especially as Chancellor of the Exchequer, Lloyd George also came to appreciate the power and generosity of the English bourgeoisie. Its Liberal section embraced the Welsh Liberal establishment as junior partners in the British and imperial enterprise, rewarding them for their loyal service with jobs, honours and some gestures of recognition towards Welsh nationality. From his elevated vantage point, Lloyd George came to realise how ruthless the British ruling class could be in pursuit of its vital interests. He understood that, under the pressure of increasingly unfavourable economic and political circumstances, there were powerful elements in the business world, in government, in the judiciary and the armed forces who would use all necessary force to crush strikes in major industries. Such methods – even when used against colonial peoples – offended the sensibilities of many Welsh petty bourgeois Liberals nurtured, as they had been, in a culture that lauded pacifism, co-operation and democracy. Nor would brutal class conflict, with a Liberal government siding openly with the employers against labour, assist the petty bourgeoisie's political hegemony in south Wales. Hence the herculean efforts of Lloyd George to settle the rail disputes of 1907 and 1911, at the expense of the workers if necessary. With the trades unions stronger and more militant than ever in the summer of 1911, he saw disaster facing his party and his class in the event of unbridled class warfare.

Lloyd George confided these fears in a note to Elizabeth Asquith, the prime minister's daughter, shortly after the railway settlement:

> I am delighted the struggle is over. I was genuinely afraid of the 'river of blood' between Liberalism and Labour. We ought to thank God that Labour had no daring leader otherwise British Liberalism could have become what Continental Liberalism now is – a respectable middle-class affair – futile and impotent. [4]

Winston Churchill represented the hard face of the British bourgeois class. Had it not been for Lloyd George's victorious efforts at conciliation, the Home Secretary's strategy would have been unleashed to the full. The likely outcome would have been a bloody defeat for the workers, with the Tories winning the next general election as Labour took votes and seats from the Liberals. Churchill's predilections can be gleaned from his response to the news that the railway strike had come to an end. He told Lloyd George on the telephone: 'I'm very sorry to hear it. It would have been better to have gone on and given these men a good thrashing'. [5] He then strode from the room to play a round of golf.

Churchill was staying at the country mansion of the Masterman family at the time; Charles Masterman was a friend and fellow minister in the government. His wife Lucy kept a detailed diary which recorded the views of both men about Churchill's conduct during the railway strike: 'He [Churchill] enjoyed immensely mapping the country and directing the movement of troops. Charlie thinks that in the main he did right, but that he did it in an amazingly wrong way, issuing wild bulletins and longing for 'blood' ... Winston was wildly excited and issued disastrous bulletins which did so much to exasperate the men's unions'. [6]

The attitude of king George V was not much more conciliatory. He told Churchill by telegram on August 16, on the eve of the strike: 'Strongly deprecate the half-hearted employment of troops. They should not be called upon except as a last resource, but if called upon they should be given a free hand and the mob should be made to fear them'. [7]

For his part, Lloyd George knew only too well the mind of his imperial majesty. In the autumn after the angry summer, he stayed as Chancellor with George V at Balmoral, from where he wrote to his wife Margaret:

> I shall be so glad to find myself in the car starting [back]. I am not cut out for Court life. I can see some of them revel in it. *I detest it.* The whole atmosphere reeks with Toryism. I can breathe it and it depresses & sickens me. Everybody very civil to me as they would be to a dangerous wild animal whom they fear & perhaps just a little admire for its suppleness & strength. The King is hostile to the bone to all who are working to lift the workmen out of the mire. So is the Queen. They talk exactly as the late King [Edward VII] & the Kaiser talked to me if you can remember the old Railway strike. 'What do they want striking?' 'They are very well paid' etc. [8]

How different from the enthusiasm of Jimmy H Thomas for the pomp, status and flummery of the royal court, and indeed for the friendship of the king himself. Throughout the Cambrian dispute, George V had expressed his concern for the 300 mules left underground at Clydach Vale. There is no record of any royal sympathy

finds it most difficult tosubject the masses morally …
*I recently read an article in an English magazine by a Tory, a political opponent of Lloyd George, entitled 'Lloyd George from the Standpoint of a Tory'. The war opened the eyes of this opponent and made him realise what an excellent servant of the bourgeoisie this Lloyd George is! The Tories have made peace with him! [14]

By the time Lenin's article was published two months later, Lloyd George had replaced Herbert Asquith as Britain's prime minister and war leader, thanks to the machinations of Tory leader Bonar Law and such Liberal capitalists as coalowner David Davies.

Back in Wales, Lloyd George and many other Liberals presented themselves to the people as 'Welsh Nationalists'. Among their patriotic causes were Disestablishment of the Anglican Church in Wales and the creation of Welsh national institutions and a Welsh education system. Support for a Welsh Parliament or 'home rule' was optional, although all Liberal 'Welsh Nationalists' paid due obeisance to king, empire and the union with England. Towards the end of the 19th century, the patriotic, democratic and radical content of Welsh Liberalism had attracted many miners' leaders to the party. The god-fearing and respectable trades unionism of such Fed officials as Mabon and Thomas Richards posed no threat to capitalism or the establishment, industrially or politically.

The real danger to the Liberal ascendancy in Wales – and to the Liberal and Tory coalowners in particular – came from the militants who agitated for industrial action, and from the socialists who were mostly organised in the ILP. These 'extreme' elements also argued for the forces of labour to break with Liberalism and form their own political party in parliament – a Labour Party. Their case was strengthened by the actions of the coalowners and railway directors, indeed by the logic of the class struggle, which drove growing numbers of 'non-political' trades unionists to the same conclusion. In 1908, the south Wales miners reversed their earlier opposition and voted to affiliate the Miners' Federation of Great Britain to the new Labour Party, compelling reluctant 'Lib-lab' union leaders to cross the parliamentary floor.

In the first decade of the century, trade union membership doubled in Britain, while the number of ILP branches in Wales rose from 27 in 1905 to 104 by 1910. [15] The response of such Welsh Liberal MPs as J Hugh Edwards, Clement Edwards and Edgar

Jones was to launch the Anti-Socialist Union. From 1907, they stumped the south Wales valleys sounding the alarm about socialism, a creed which supposedly intended to destroy religion and the family, and to tear the Welsh nation in two by setting worker against employer. They claimed that socialist ideas were alien to Welsh temperament and tradition, and were preached mainly by infidel *'dieithriaid'* ('strangers') and *'estronwyr'* ('foreigners') – well understood code words in the Welsh language for 'the English'. David Thomas of Talysarn replied that Christianity had come from Palestine, Protestantism from Germany and Calvinism from Geneva; but he also urged the socialist movement to immerse itself in the national language, history and traditions of Welsh working people. [16]

Keir Hardie embodied everything that was so so detested by the Anti-Socialist Union. He was the first and most prominent socialist MP of the time, founder of the ILP and the Labour Party, the driving force of the *Labour Leader and Merthyr Pioneer* and, in the words of the Rev. WF Phillips, arch-priest of the anti-socialist crusade, 'the narrow and unpatriotic foreigner who, alas, represents Merthyr Boroughs'. [17]

Throughout the summer of 1911, Hardie had infuriated 'Welsh Nationalists' with his jibes at the July investiture of the young Edward as 'Prince of Wales', an extravagant jamboree orchestrated by Lloyd George himself. While the self-appointed patriots clamoured to crown an Anglo-German aristocrat, they heaped scorn upon the impudent Scot who sang *'Mae Hen Wlad Fy Nhadau'* in Welsh alongside *'The Red Flag'*. Hardie recalled that the first prince of Wales had been imposed on a conquered and dispossessed people by an English king and his robber barons. [18] He told a May Day rally in Tonypandy that this latest investiture 'ought to make every Welshman who was patriotic blush with shame'; for his part, Hardie had no intention to attend at Caernarfon castle, although 'every flunkey in Wales, Liberal and Tory alike, is grovelling on his hands and knees to take part in the ceremony'. [19]

Likewise, Keir Hardie hurled the licenced 'patriotism' of the Welsh Liberals back in their faces in the case of the Llanelli killings. He told a large meeting at the Market Hall, Llanelli, shortly after the fateful events that 'Welsh nationalism was all very well at election times, but it was a very spurious kind of nationalism that allowed English soldiers to shoot Welshmen without any protest'. [20] He made the same point in a series of speeches across south Wales that autumn, culminating in his proclamation of an alternative type of Welsh nationalism in a speech in Dowlais, on October 7:

They were hearing about Welsh Nationalism. Being a Scotsman, he believed in nationality. But they should be aware that nationalism was the genuine article, and not some spurious imitation. They had members of their Nationalist party going about in Wales making speeches: they had been talking about Welsh Nationalism; had they heard one of them offer one single word of sympathy or compassion to the old mother and father who were crying their hearts out in the lonely home in Llanelly for the Welsh lads who were shot through the heart? Not one. They talked of Welsh nationalism when they wanted votes, but when it came to doing anything for the workers they were not nationalists, they were not even Welshmen, they were simply party politicians intent upon keeping the workers in their rightful place. (Loud applause). 'Men and women of Dowlais', declared Mr Keir Hardie, 'we are going to have a Welsh Nationalist Party, and if Sir Alfred Mond can lead the "Nationalist" Party in Wales at present, it is quite possible that Keir Hardie will lead the real party. (Loud and prolonged cheering). The Nationalist Party I have in mind is this: the people of Wales fighting to recover possession of the land of Wales – (hear, hear) – the working class of Wales acquiring possession of the the mines, of the furnaces, and the railways, of the great public works generally, and working them as comrades, not for the benefit of shareholders, but for the good of every man, woman, and child within your borders. (Loud cheers). That is the kind of Nationalism that I want to see brought about. And when that comes the red dragon will be emblazoned on the red flag of Socialism, the international emblem of the working class movement throughout the world'. (Loud and prolonged cheers). [21]

The Welsh 'nationalism' of Lloyd George and the Welsh Liberals actually represented the class interests, primarily, of the Welsh petty bourgeoisie, the self-employed small property owners in town and country, and notably of its intelligentsia; but it also expressed the aspirations of a national identity that the Welsh petty bourgeoisie had played the leading role in defining and constructing.

But Welsh Liberalism also comprised a cohort of big capitalists, whose real 'compatriots' were the Liberal coalowners, manufacturers and shipping magnates of England rather than the preachers and lawyers of Wales. Increasingly, therefore, Welsh Liberalism's 'Welsh Nationalism' degenerated into an ideology of class collaboration with – and surrender to – monopoly capitalism, to be propagated among the Welsh working class in the name of a spurious Welsh Christian tradition and 'national unity' against socialism. For Welsh petty bourgeois politicians, Liberalism became the vehicle for self-advancement in the service of British capitalism and imperialism.

Keir Hardie and others in the Welsh labour movement glimpsed the potential for redefining Welsh nationalism, giving it an egalitarian and republican content that would be in the interests of the working class. However, this approach was never adopted consistently by the labour movement, which quickly came to believe that the national question had no progressive role to play in 20th century Wales.

An echo of the Llanelli killings and the political climate in which they occurred was soon to be heard in the popular contemporary stage drama, *'Change'*, by JO Francis. [22] Although Francis set the action in a fictional coal mining village in Glamorgan, the essential features of the story are based on the bloody events in Llanelli. A strike is in progress, with strikers and their supporters gathering to stop a train-load of strike-breakers and soldiers when the engine slows at a railway crossing. Troops have mustered to protect the train, precipitating clashes with the picketers. Gwilym Price, a well-regarded, local young man is visiting a friend whose house overlooks the scene; stones thrown from its rear garden have struck some of the soldiers. One protestor is not worried about the possibility of lethal retaliation – he tells the crowd that the troops can only fire blanks. Gwilym has clambered onto a wall, trying to pull his militant brother, Lewis, out of the firing line. Then, after a warning, the soldiers open fire. Gwilym is mortally wounded by the volley, and is carried into the house.

As in other dramas by JO Francis, much of the dialogue reflects the political conflict of the time between Welsh Nonconformist Liberalism and secular, class-struggle Socialism – with an intelligent central character who is torn apart by contradictory loyalties, and usually ends up trying to escape through drink, emigration or both. In one scene, Lewis Price is arguing with his father, who is a chapel deacon and collier of the old school:

> Labour and Capital are at grips, always, always! Whether we're working or whether we're striking, we're fighting that battle, day by day and hour by hour. And you're not in the fighting line. You're prisoners of the past. It's tied your hands and it's blinded your eyes ... All along you've been waiting and compromising. You called yourselves 'Liberal-Labour'. Even your very name was

compromise – and that's why you've never, never done anything at all ... Men were never more earnest than they are now. There's something stirring in the dark. All over the wide earth it's stirring, and there's nothing can keep it still. Call it Socialism, Syndicalism, unrest or revolution. Call it what you like. But it's the worker coming to his own at last through suffering and through struggle ... But you're not with us. You're looking back; we're looking forward. And, because you're looking back, you can't understand what's going on about you day by day.

Yet neither the labour movement nor the socialists within it were able to utilise the events in Llanelli effectively, for their cause. No mobilising 'myth' could be created around the 'Llanelli martyrs'. The subsequent by election failures have already been recounted. The efforts of Victor Grayson and the British Socialist Party to set up a local branch in the autumn of 1911 came to nought. Nor would there be any delayed-action benefits in the longer-term. Although Labour's vote in the Llanelli district rose steadily in succeeding years, culminating in the victory of Dr John Williams in the 1923 general election, this merely conformed to the pattern across industrial Wales. Between 1918 and 1923, a political revolution occurred at parliamentary and municipal levels, with the Labour Party replacing the Liberals as the party of the Welsh industrial proletariat and working people generally.

The labour movement in Wales had neither the Welsh historical class consciousness, nor the organisational means at the national all-Wales level, to produce and utilise its own history. The study and manufacture of Welsh history was only just beginning to be rescued from Celtic antiquarianism; and the first modern Welsh historians – products of Oxford University and the fledgling University of Wales – were Liberal, petty bourgeois and 'Welsh Nationalist' in their outlook and preoccupations.

Not until the mid-1920s, when future MP Ness Edwards produced his histories of industrialisation and the south Wales miners, did the Welsh working class have access to substantial accounts of its own past written from a 'class struggle' perspective. [23] Edwards was a product of the Central Labour College in London, established in 1913 jointly by the National Union of Railwaymen and the South Wales Miners Federation. Hundreds of Welsh workers went there to study the history of the labour and socialist movements, Marxist political economy, literature and a range of other subjects – but none of them in relation to Wales. Organisationally, the Welsh working class exercised little or no autonomy that could be used to commemorate, record and proclaim its own experience: most trades unionists were in centralised British trades unions by the turn of the century; there was some Welsh autonomy in the ILP, but none of any substance in the Labour Party; the existence of north and south Wales labour federations from 1914 was sporadic, and attempts to fuse them into a single all-Wales Labour Party organisation were frustrated from London. [24] Even the Welsh labour and socialist press went into terminal decline between 1914 and 1929. Formerly the most influential of the weekly papers, *Llais Llafur ('Labour Voice')* retreated back to the Tawe valley as a local and largely non-political news sheet: the *South Wales Voice*. Aberdare's *Tarian y Gweithwyr ('The Workers' Shield')* went from being a 'Lib-lab' paper for south Wales to a religious and local journal for the Cynon valley, before being swallowed by the Aberdare Leader.

To some extent, the south Wales miners and their union withstood these tendencies to centralisation and anglicisation. The 'Fed' retained substantial powers and resources of its own, and its affiliated lodges, combines and 'unofficial' committees published a range of news and propaganda papers – especially in periods of heightened class conflict. Here a specifically Welsh (or more precisely, a peculiarly 'South Walian') historical class consciousness did develop, especially around the Chartists and the struggles of the miners themselves. Even so, the traumatic killings in Llanelli were rarely if ever recalled by any section of the Welsh labour movement in later decades. The graves of John John and Leonard Worsell were allowed to fall into disrepair, the inscriptions on their headstones to fade and crumble. There has been no memorial plaque or monument. No books, pamphlets, television or radio programmes about the events appeared until the 1980s. The first march and rally to remember the two men did not take place until 1981, and then it was initiated not by any section of the official labour movement, but by the short-lived Welsh Socialist Republican Movement. If there are references to the Llanelli events in the history books, they are often erroneous. The enormity of what happened in August 1911 has rarely if ever been taught in schools, within or beyond the town and its hinterland. As Marx and Engels observed: 'The ruling ideas of each age have ever been the ideas of its ruling class'. [25]

This is true of ideas about history, about what is investigated and presented in the present about the past. Yet the working class and its labour movement have produced ideas to challenge those of the capitalist class, including a working class view of history. In Wales, for example, the past struggles of the Chartists, the miners and the quarryworkers have been studied and presented extensively in the closing decades of the 20th century, and from a sympathetic standpoint. The silence shrouding the events in Llanelli is only partly explained by the hegemony of capitalist ideology.

There are other – sectional and local – factors to be taken into account. Firstly, like other sections of the workforce in south Wales, the railway workers have been marginalised even in the field of Welsh labour history by the overpowering presence of the coal miners. Understandably, given their weight in economic, social and political life, many more books have been written about the south Wales miners and their leaders than about all the other contingents of the region's working class put together. Secondly, Llanelli's position on the edge of the coalfield, dominated by a tinplate industry that has itself generated little interest among labour historians, has helped to obscure the scale and significance of its part in the conflict of 1911. This obscurity has, of course, been aided and abetted by a respectable Liberal – and later Labour – municipal establishment anxious to dispel any image of Llanelli as a riotous storm-centre of class struggle. Nor, in truth, was it ever such a centre except for those few days in August. The drama of that episode left little imprint on the labour movement and Welsh politics, except in one quarter – among the Llanelli railway workers themselves.

The local branches of the NUR and footplate workers' union ASLEF quickly developed a reputation for almost unparalleled militancy. When Dublin transport workers were locked out by intransigent employers in November 1913, the Llanelli railwaymen joined trades unionists in Liverpool, Birmingham and Yorkshire in taking solidarity action. They were protesting against the inactivity of the British Trades Union Congress. On November 7, driver George James refused to shunt a train laden with Dublin cargo at Llandeilo Junction and was soon suspended and then sacked. A member of the NUR executive warned the press:

> Llanelly is the one district in South Wales where we have had the most trouble recently. The men there are the most advanced in our ranks, and some of them would strike on the slightest pretext. I know that all over the country there are thousands of railwaymen eagerly awaiting a chance for showing their sympathy with the Dublin workers, and this Llanelly incident will give them all they ask for. [26]

A few days later and in solidarity with his colleague, driver Reynolds refused to work and was subsequently dismissed. Official ASLEF and unofficial NUR strikes broke out across south Wales against the sackings, with future ASLEF general secretary Richard Squance in the vanguard. Eventually, NUR president JH Thomas negotiated a separate and complex settlement with Great Western Railways for his union's own members which included a 'no victimisation' clause and improved working hours. [27] ASLEF action won complete reinstatement for James and lapsed member Reynolds. [28]

James and Reynolds were – like John John and Leonard Worsell – privates in the industrial army. But they were also in that part of the army which was developing a 'political' dimension to its class consciousness. They understood that the class struggle occurred independently of the wishes, of the awareness even, of individual workers. James and Reynolds would have agreed with Lewis Price, the collier in 'Change' who had been educated by the class struggle and the Plebs League: 'As long as Labour and Capital exist as they do now, you must stir up strife – all over the place'. There are often casualties when the class struggle takes the form of open class warfare, people such as John and Worsell and their families. Yet capitalism produces more than enough casualties in times of comparative class 'peace' as well.

Notes

Chapter 1: Railwaymen

1. *Although the new Act granted unions immunity from some aspects of common law when engaged in a legitimate trade dispute, it did not provide for immunity from the criminal law or from common law in general. For a lucid and comprehensive account of the legal position of trades unions during this period, see for example GDH Cole, A Short History of the British Working-Class Movement (1947) pp.296-305.*
2. *Llais Llafur, August 24, 1907.*
3. *Llais Llafur, October 19, 1907.*
4. *George Dangerfield, The Strange Death of Liberal England (1936) p.31.*
5. *'Y mae efe, fel Burns, wedi ei brynu gorff, enaid a chyneddfau gan Rhyddfrydiaeth swyddogol, am ddwy fil o bunau yn flynyddol; nid yw bellach ond cynffon, a rhaid i'r gynffon siglo yn ol mympwy ac wrth ewyllys y ci a'i perchnoga', (Llais Llafur, October 5, 1907). John Burns MP had been a militant trade union leader before turning away from socialism and the labour movement; he took a post in Campbell-Bannerman's Liberal government in 1906.*
6. *For most of these statistics and their sources see Philip S Bagwell, The Railwaymen: The History of the National Union of Railwaymen (1963) p.262. Figures relating to pay, working hours and accidents were collected by the Amalgamated Society of Railway Servants in 1907 for its renowned 'Green Book'; results from this survey were published widely in the press, including the South Wales Daily News, November 4, 1907.*
7. *B Mitchell and P Deane eds., Abstract of British Historical Statistics (1962) pp.225-27*
8. *See D Tudwal Evans, Sosialaeth (1911) p.81, where he cites statistics from William Cunningham, Should our railways be nationalised? (1906).*
9. *Evans (1911) pp.86-7.*
10. *'The National All-Grades Programme was reprinted in the Report of the Royal Commission on the Railway Conciliation and Arbitration Scheme of*

1907' (Command 5922, 1911) p.6.

11. The ASLEF programme is summarised in Robert Griffiths, *Driven by Ideals: A History of ASLEF* (2005) pp.39-40, together with an account of the conflict between the rail unions during this period.

12. *Llais Llafur*, September 21, 1907.

13. 'Beth sydd angen ynte? Cenedlaetholi y rheilffyrdd; y wlad i berchenogi ffrwyth llafur ei meibion ... Ond cyhyd ag y byddo gwyr ein rheilffyrdd mor ynfyd ag anfon cyfarwyddwyr Rhyddfrydol a Thoriaidd i'w cynrychioli yn St. Stephan, a Richard Bell a'i gyffelyb i ymbil am friwsion oddiar fwrdd gwladwriaethol Westminster, ac i dynu eu hetiau yn ostyngedig i ysbeilwyr trwsiadus, a llechu tan aden yr un blaid a hwythau, cyhyd a hyny y byddant heb symud gam ym mlaen yn nghyfeiriad eu rhyddhad o'u llyffeitheiriau; cyhyd y rhaid iddynt floeddio yn ofer, am rhyw beth gwell na deg awr y dydd, a phunt yr wythnos o gyflog. Nid oes ond un llwybr iachawdwriaeth, sef taflu y Richard Bells a'r Lib-Labs eraill o'r neilldu, ac ymlwybro ym mlaen i fuddugoliaeth ac hapusrwydd dan faner fendigedig Cymdeithasiaeth. Rhaid dewis yn arweinwyr yr Hardies a'r Hyndmans, ac ymwrthod am byth a'r Bells a'r Maddisons. A rhaid chwynu peth ar blaid Anibynol Llafur hefyd, cyn y daw yn offeryn cymhwys i'r gwaith anrhaethadwy bwysig sydd o'i blaen, ac yn aros ei gyflawniad'. (Llais Llafur, September 21, 1907), Fred Maddison was a typesetter by craft and an MP 1897-1900 and 1906-10. HM Hyndman was leader of the Marxist-oriented Social Democratic Federation which he helped to found in 1884; he later became the leader of the British Socialist Party, the product of a merger in 1911, before resigning in 1916 because of his jingoistic position on the 1914-18 imperialist war.

14. Quoted from the Campbell-Bannerman papers in the British Museum, in Peter Rowland, *Lloyd George* (1975) p.194.

15. See note 6 above.

16. Bagwell (1963) p. 272; *Manchester Guardian*, August 18, 1907; CJ Wrigley, *Lloyd George and the British Labour Movement* (1976) pp.50-58.

17. George Askwith, *Industrial Problems and Disputes* (1920) p.126.

18. *South Wales Daily News*, November 12, 1907.

19. *Llais Llafur*, November 9, 1907.

20. *South Wales Daily News*, November 8 and 9, 1907.

21. *South Wales Daily News, November 8, 1907.*
22. *VI Lenin, 'Trade Union Neutrality', published originally in Proletary, March 3, 1908 and reprinted in Collected Works Vol. 13 (1962) pp.468-9 and in On Britain (1973) pp.80-81. James Burnett was Secretary of the Scottish Council of the SDF. Marshal Francois Bazaine commanded the Army of the Rhine in the Franco-Prussian War and surrendered at Metz in October 1870; after the Battle of Sedan, in September 1870, Napolean III surrendered to the Prussians.*
23. *The details of this and other settlements during the period can be found in the 'Railway Conciliation Scheme: Statement of Settlements etc.' issued by the Board of Trade (Command 5332, 1910).*

Chapter 2: The Baptists' Jerusalem

1. *South Wales Daily News, October 28, 1907.*
2. *South Wales Daily News, November 4, 1907.*
3. *Y Diwygiwr, March 1844.*
4. *'Yr amgylchiadau galarus, gresynol a gwarthus a gymerasant le yn ddiweddar, ydynt yn galw arnom i derfynu'n hysgrif Siartiaidd yn wahanol iawn i'r hyn a arfaethasom wneuthur. Bwriadem gynnig ychydig sylwadau cydlawenychol a'n brodyr o bob gradd, am y tybiem fod yr egwyddori teuluol, yr addysgu Sabothol, y teimladau crefyddol, a'r wybodaeth wleidiadol a feddyliem fod yn ffynnu, fel cynifer o warchgloddiau rhwng y Cymry byth a rhedeg i'r unrhyw eithafoedd rhyfygus, anghrefyddol, ac annynol, a dynionach gwamal ac ansefydlog Ffrainc, a gwerinos anwybodus ac anghrefyddol Manchester a Birmingham. Nid oedd dim yn sicrach gennym na bod digon o wybodaeth wleidiadol, synnwyr naturiol, a theimladau crefyddol yng ngwlad ein genedigaeth i rwystro unrhyw ddosbarth ohoni i liwio'i gweryd a gwaed, ac i fod yn gyfrannog mewn gwrthryfel mor ddwl, ynfyd, a di-reswm, nac i ymuno mewn ymgyrch mor elynol i drefn wladol, mor ddinistriol i ddedwyddwch cymdeithasol, i gysur teuluol, ac i bob teimlad a'n harddurnant fel dynion ac fel Cristnogion; ond yr ydym wedi'n siomi – mae'n gwlad wedi ei gwarthnodi – mae'n cenedl dan warth – tebygol fod degau wedi eu lladd, ac ychwaneg wedi eu clwyfo o'r rhai a ddygent yr enw 'Terfysgwyr',*

mae gweddwon tirion a'u gruddiau'n wlybion oherwydd i'r gwyr syrthio yn y terfysg, mae plant bychain amddifad yn cwyno oherwydd i'w tadau syrthio i'r bedd yn amhrydlon, llawer Rahel sydd yn awr yng Nghymru yn wylo am eu plant, ac ni fynnant eu cysuro. Yn y Casnewydd yng Nghymru mae arogl y pylor dinistriol heb fyned heibio, ac anghyfanhedd-dra erchyll rhyfel gartrefol i'w weled ... Wel, i ba beth yr aethant i Gasnewydd, ac o flaen y milwyr fel defaid i'r lladdfa? Amlwg ydyw mai eu llithio gadd rhai gan siaradwyr diegwyddor a hunanol, a chael eu dylanwadu gadd eraill gan eu cyfeillion, a'u gorfodi gadd y rhan amlaf o lawer. Hyderir y bydd y fath amgylchiad gresynol yn rhybudd effeithiol i'r werin i brofi'r ysbrydoedd, ac i fod ar eu gwyliadwriaeth, rhag cael eu twyllo a'u hud-ddenu gan ddynion awyddus i fod yn rhywbeth ar draul a gwasanaeth eraill ...' (Y Diwygiwr, December 1839).

5. *'Y peth cyntaf a'm tarawodd ydoedd y ffyrdd bydron, y mwg afiach a'r tram yn cael ei dynu gan un ceffyl. Mae'r tram cul yn cael ei dynu gan geffyl main yn werth edrych arno. Dyma un o hen bethau'r cyn-oesoedd, dyma grair gwerth ei gadw a'i osod yn Ngheirfa Genedlaethol Cymru pan y sefydlir hi, ac ar ol i Lanelli dyfu allan o'r cyflwr barbaraidd sydd yn gwneuthur y peth hyn yn bosibl ... Am y mwg, wrth gwrs nis gellir osgoi hwn, cyhyd ag y bo'r holl weithiau alcam, dur etc. wedi eu planu yng nghanol y lle, a'r tai wedi eu codi yn grynswth direol o'u cwmpas. O ryfedd anrhefn afiach. Beth barodd i drefniadau disynwyr a hyn gymeryd lle sydd yn hynod i ni heddyw. Y mae'n rhyfedd fod iechyd y bobl cystal ag y mae o dan amgylchoedd mor niweidiol'. ('Trwy Spectol Gweinidog' [Through a Minister's Spectacles]: 'Cwrs y Byd' [The Way of the World] in Llais Llafur, September 14, 1907).*

6. *Llais Llafur, September 14, 1907.*

7. *Deian Hopkin, 'The Rise of Labour: Llanelli, 1890-1922' in Geraint H Jenkins & J Beverley Smith eds., Politics and Society in Wales, 1840-1922: Essays in Honour of Ieuan Gwynedd Jones (1988).*

8. *Idris C. Bell, 'The Tinplate Workers Union' in Goronwy Alun Hughes ed., Men of No Property (1972); see also Philip J. Leng, The Welsh Dockers (1981) for the history of the dock and tinplate workers in south Wales.*

9. *Llais Llafur, October 5, 1907.*

10. *Llanelly Mercury, August 24, 1911.*

11. *South Wales Press, November 16, 1910.*
12. *War Office papers relating to Harold Spiers, WO 97/5973/XP/002748, Public Record Office.*

Chapter 3: The Great Strike

1. *Philip S Bagwell, The Railwaymen: The History of the National Union of Railwaymen (1963) p.286.*
2. *'Conciliation or Emancipation' in the Industrial Syndicalist, May 1911.*
3. *Bagwell (1963) pp.284, 289. The Annual Reports of the Board of Trade on Changes in Wages and Hours are a valuable source of information in these areas; they also confirm the accuracy of the 1907 ASRS Green Book survey.*
4. *The Parliamentary Debates (Official Report), Fifth series, Vol. XXI, House of Commons, col.239 (February 7, 1911).*
5. *Merthyr Express, November 19, 1910.*
6. *South Wales Daily News, August 11, 1911.*
7. *South Wales Daily News, August 17, 1911.*
8. *Official Report Vol. XXIX col.2336 (August 22, 1911). Sir Guy Granet's disowned remarks were published in numerous newspapers including the Daily Mail, August 17, 1911, and the Railway Gazette, August 18, 1911; Granet's letter on this matter is reprinted in Randolph S Churchill, Winston S. Churchill: Companion Vol. II Part 2, 1907-1911 (1969) pp. 1277-78.*
9. *Official Report, Vol. XXIX cols.2046-8 (August 16, 1911).*
10. *See Bagwell (1963) p.295.*
11. *General Sir Nevil Macready, Annals of an Active Life Vol. I (1924) p.163.*
12. *Ramsay MacDonald recounted this episode in the House of Commons on August 22, 1911 (Official Report, Vol. XXIX cols. 2351-2); accounts of the discussions between the unions, the Government and the employers can be found in Bagwell (1963), Rowland (1975), Dangerfield (1936) and – in the right chronological order – Gregory Blaxland, JH Thomas: A Life for Unity (1964) pp.72-6.*
13. *George Askwith, Industrial Problems and Disputes (1920) p.164*
14. *Griffiths (2005) p.53; Bagwell (1963) p.294.*
15. *Churchill (1969) pp.1278-79*

16. *The Story of the Great Railway Strike (1911) p.5, a series of reports reprinted from the Cambria Daily Leader.*

17. *South Wales Daily News, August 21, 1911.*

18. *Masterman (1939) pp.207-8.*

19. *Randolph S. Churchill (1969) pp. 1271-72; Granet's allegations were contained in a letter to Winston Churchill dated August 15, 1911. Sir Almeric Fitzroy reported in his Memoirs (1925) that Churchill believed and helped circulate these stories.*

20. *Westminster Gazette, August 19, 1911.*

21. *Churchill (1969) pp.1287-88.*

22. *K. O. Morgan ed., Lloyd George: Family Letters 1885-1936 (1973) p.158*

23. *Austen Chamberlain, Politics from the Inside (1936) pp.320, 437.*

24. *Askwith (1920) p. 166; Mary Hamilton, Arthur Henderson (1938) pp.87-88.*

25. *Randolph S. Churchill, Winston S. Churchill: Companion Vol. II Part 2, 1907-1911 (1969) p.1128.*

26. *Official Report, Vol. XXXII col.131 (November 27, 1911).*

27. *Labour Leader, March 13, 1913.*

28. *Railway News, August 26, 1911.*

29. *Official Report, Vol. XXIX cols. 2317-8 (August 22, 1911)*

30. *Llanelly Mercury, August 24, 1911*

31. *The Times, August 21, 1911*

32. *Merthyr Pioneer, August 26, 1911*

33. *Royal Archives, RA/B246(20), British Museum*

34. *Randolph S. Churchill, Winston S. Churchill: Young Statesman 1901-14 (1967) pp.385-86*

Chapter 4: The Shooting

1. *Llais Llafur, August 12, 1911.*

2. *This estimate is based on local press reports and taken from Deian Hopkin, 'The Llanelli Riots, 1911' in the Welsh History Review Vol. 11 No. 4, December 1983.*

3. *South Wales Press, August 16, 1911.*

4. *Llanelly Mercury, August 24, 1911.*

5. *Home Office papers, HO 45/10658/212470/171, Public Record Office*

6. *The account of events in this chapter draws heavily from the reports in the South Wales Daily News, Llanelly Mercury and South Wales Daily Press; from the Report of the Chief Constable of Carmarthenshire to the Standing Joint Committee of the County Council, reprinted in the Llanelly Mercury, October 12, 1911; and from reports of the inquest proceedings in the Llanelly Mercury, August 13 and 31, 1911, South Wales Daily News, August 30, 1911 and Western Mail, August 30, 1911.*

7. *Chief Constable's Report (see note 6 above).*

8. *HO 45/10654/212470/105.*

9. *South Wales Press, August 23, 1911.*

10. *The Story of the Great Railway Strike (1911) p.6, a series of reports reprinted from the Cambria Daily Leader.*

11. *HO 45/10658/212470/206.*

12. *Western Mail, August 21, 1911.*

13. *Llanelly Mercury, August 31, 1911.*

14. *South Wales Daily News, August 22, 1911.*

15. *Quoted by Dr T. Reginald Davies in article by Harry Davies in the Llanelli Star, August 22, 1981; Dr Davies also recalled this incident in 'Y Gwrthgiliwr' ('The Deserter'), a drama-documentary programme broadcast on Sianel Pedwar Cymru (S4C) television on August 11, 1983.*

16. *Llanelly Mercury, August 24, 1911.*

17. *This allegation was recalled by Dr T. Reginald Davies (see note 15 above); one eye-witness, Llewellyn Phillips of 99 Station Rd., Llanelli, told the inquest that the engine driver was so much under the influence of drink that he was 'unable to walk without assistance' (Llanelly Mercury, August 31, 1911).*

18. *Western Mail, August 21, 1911.*

19. *Llanelly Mercury, August 24, 1911.*

Chapter 5: A Heavy Reckoning

1. *Report of the Chief Constable to the Standing Joint Committee, published in the Llanelly Mercury, October 12, 1911.*

2. *South Wales Daily News, August 21, 1911.*

3. *The Story of the Great Railway Strike (1911) p.9.*

4. *The Story of the Great Railway Strike (1911) p.10.*

5. *Llanelly Mercury, August 24, 1911.*

6. *Llanelly Mercury, August 24, 1911.*

7. *Llanelly Mercury, August 24, 1911.*

8. *Llanelly Mercury, August 24, 1911.*

9. *Dr. T. Reginald Davies, quoted by Harry Davies in the Llanelli Star, August 22, 1911.*

10. *The Times, August 21, 1911.*

11. *South Wales Press, August 23, 1911.*

12. *Official Report, Vol. XXIX col. 2332 (August 22, 1911).*

13. *The Times, August 21, 1911.*

14. *Cited in 'The Month in Wales' by the editor, J. Hugh Edwards, in Wales, September 1911.*

15. *Llais Llafur, September 2, 1911.*

16. *'Y mae prif dref yr alcanwyr yng Nghymru, sef Llanelli, wedi hynodi ei hun yn ystod streic a rheilffyrddwyr, ac y mae y trigolion wedi dwyn y dref o dan warth, ac o hyn allan ni adwaenir y dref fel tref heddychol, ond fel trigfa terfysgwyr, lladron a meddwon. Y mae yn resyn fod y fath enw wedi ei ddwyn arni gan dorf o hwliganiaid diwaith, a segurwyr ystwrllyd'. (Tarian y Gweithiwr, August 24, 1911).*

17. *Llanelly Mercury, August 24, 1911.*

18. *'Ni phetruswn ddweud mai gwaith dosparth o hwliganiaid annuwiol a diog yw y rhan fwyaf o'r difrod a'r yspeilio a'r llosgi. Na feier holl bobl Llanelli na Lerpwl am y galanastra, oddigerth ar y tir y dylai efallai corff mawr y bobl dawel a da gymeryd mesurau mwy pendant i atal rhwysg anarchiaeth yn eu misg. Credwn yn sicr y byddai catrawd o ddineswyr parchus a chrefyddol yn llawer mwy llwyddiannus ac effeithiol i gadw'r heddwch na milwyr a phlismyn. Nid y streicwyr sydd yn gwneud y difrod, ond 'rebals' ac ysgubion sydd pob amser yn barod i fanteisio ar unrhyw gyfle i gyflawni trosedd'. ('Y Streic a'i Wersi' ['The Strike and its Lessons'] in Y Tyst, August 23, 1911).*

19. *'Y mae miloedd pobl oreu Llanelli yn fawr eu condemniad ar fechgynos*

anghyfrifol, a llawer o ddyiethriaid daeth i'r dref i weithio yn ddiweddar am dynu enw da y dref i lawr, ac nid oes yma rith o gydymdeimlad na chefnogaeth i'r lladrata ynfyd ac anrheithio dibris gymerodd le. Na feier ond gwehilion y dref am bethau fel hyn'. ('Pob Ochr i'r Heol' ['Each Side of the Road' – a regular column] in Y Tyst, August 30, 1911).

20. Llanelly and County Guardian, August 31, 1911.

21. 'The Month in Wales', Wales, September 1911.

22. This information was collated from the local press and court records by Deian Hopkin for his article 'The Llanelli Riots, 1911' in the Welsh History Review, Vol. 11 No. 4, December 1983.

23. South Wales Press, August 23, 1911.

24. See Hopkin (1983) p. 501, with sources.

25. Official Report, Vol. XXIX cols. 2334-5 (August 22, 1911).

26. 'Mae'r Cymry yn rhai brwdfrydig, ac mae eu brwdfrydedd yn mynd ar dan ac yn ffaglu mewn torf, ac yngwyneb gwrthwynebiad. Ond pe cawsid torf o Gymry yn ei phang penaf, ond ar ei phen ei hun, heb estroniaid o Saeson ac ereill yn eu cynhyrfu, buasai yn hawdd i genad hedd gael tawelwch, a buasai canu ton Gymreig gan ran o hono yn effeithiolach wed'yn ... O! mae'n biti fod y Cymry yn cael anair yn ei chyffroadau, a hyny yn herwydd estroniaid segur, di-Dduw, a dibarch at ddyn. Nid un felly yw y Cymro, ond rhai dieflig felly ydyw lliaws sydd o'i gylch, ac yn ei arwain yn ddiniwed i'w hunan-laddiad'. ('Y Cymry fel Terfysgwyr' ['The Welsh as Rioters'], Tarian y Gweithiwr, September 7, 1911).

Chapter 6: The Man with the Gun at His Side

1. The following account is drawn from reports in the Llanelly Mercury, August 31, 1911; South Wales Daily News, August 23 and 25, 1911; and the Western Mail, August 23, 25, 26 and 28, 1911.

2. Llanelly Mercury, August 31, 1911

3. South Wales Daily News, September 2, 1911

4. The poem was reprinted in the South Wales Press, September 27, 1911, together with some derogatory editorial remarks.

5. South Wales Daily News, August 30, 1911.

6. *Llanelly Mercury, August 31, 1911.*

7. *A full report of the tribunal appeared in the South Wales Press, September 27, 1911.*

8. *Home Office papers, HO 45/10656/212470/352/6634, Public Record Office*

9. *Handwritten note by Troup on a memorandum from Churchill instructing him to write to the War Office, HO 45/10656/212470/352/6634.*

10. *Llanelly Mercury, October 5, 1911.*

11. *War Office papers relating to Harold Spiers, WO 97/5973/XP/002748, Public Record Office.*

12. *See Ruth & Edmund Frow and Michael Katanka, Strikes – A Documentary History (1971) p. 148.*

13. *Official Report, Vol. XXXVI col. 109 (March 25, 1912) – Llanelli is transcribed as 'Glenetly'!*

14. *Official Report, Vol. XXXVI col. 1316 (April 10, 1912).*

15. *Information received from Desmond Spiers, nephew of Harold Spiers, in conversation and correspondence, 1983.*

Chapter 7: Killing No Murder?

1. *Llanelly and County Guardian, August 24, 1911.*

2. *'Prin y cred neb yn Llanelli yr aethai pethau agos cyn waethed onibai am ddyfodiad y lluoedd arfog i'r lle ... Diau y buasai yma gyffro a gwrthryfel yn erbyn gollwng y trens drwy'r fro, ond y saethu a fu ar ddynion diniwed yn gynar yn y prydnawn barodd i'r trefwyr golli arnynt ei hunain, a rhoi'r ffrywn i'r nwydau – taflu pob cymod a threfn i'r gwynt, ac ymollwng i derfysgu'.* ('Pob Ochr i'r Heol', Y Tyst, August 30, 1911).

3. *South Wales Press, August 23, 1911.*

4. *Llanelly Mercury, August 24, 1911.*

5. *Llanelly Mercury, August 24, 1911.*

6. *Railway Review, August 23, 1911.*

7. *South Wales Daily News, August 28, 1911.*

8. *South Wales Daily News, August 21, 1911.*

9. *K.O. Morgan ed., Lloyd George: Family Letters 1885-1936 (1973) p.158.*

10. *Llanelly Mercury, August 31, 1911.*

11. *Home Office papers, HO 45/10658/212470/224, Public Record Office.*

12. *HO 45/10658/212470/323.*

13. *This account of the inquest proceedings is drawn from reports in the Llanelly Mercury, August 31, 1911; the South Wales Press, August 30, 1911; and the Western Mail, August 30, 1911.*

14. *Llanelly Mercury, August 31, 1911.*

15. *J. Keir Hardie, Killing No Murder! – The Government and the Railway Strike (1912 edn.) p.16. The first edition of the pamphlet was published in 1911.*

16. *Reports of the march and rally can be found in the Llanelly Mercury, September 14, 1911; the South Wales Press, September 13, 1911; and the Western Mail, September 11, 1911.*

17. *Tarian y Gweithiwr, September 14, 1911.*

18. *South Wales Press, October 4, 1911.*

19. *Llanelly Mercury, October 12, 1911.*

20. *Llanelly Mercury, October 12, 1911.*

21. *South Wales Daily News, January 22, 1912.*

22. *South Wales Daily News, January 22, 1912.*

23. *Llanelly Mercury, July 31, 1914.*

24. *Llanelly Mercury, August 14, 1913.*

25. *HO 45/10658/212470/460, 462 and 468.*

26. *Report of the Royal Commission on the Railway Conciliation and Arbitration Scheme of 1907 (Command 5922, 1911).*

27. *Official Report, Vol. XXXI col. 1209 (November 22, 1911).*

28. *See Gregory Blaxland, J.H. Thomas: A Life for Unity (1964) p.81.*

29. *Philip S. Bagwell, The Railwaymen: The History of the National Union of Railwaymen (1963) p.336.*

30. *From a resolution of the NUR Annual General Meeting in June 1914, quoted in Bagwell (1963) p.307.*

Chapter 8: History as Class Struggle

1. *Karl Marx & Frederick Engels, Collected Works Vol. 6 (1976) p.489.*

2. *Marx & Engels, Collected Works Vol. 6 (1976) p.491.*
3. *From the Foreword to the 1922 French and German editions of Imperialism: the Highest Stage of Capitalism (1917); see V. I. Lenin, Collected Works Vol. 22 (1964) p.190.*
4. *John Grigg, Lloyd George: The People's Champion 1902-1911 (1978) p.293.*
5. *Lucy Masterman, C.F.G. Masterman: A Biography (1939) p.208.*
6. *Masterman (1939) pp.205-6.*
7. *Randolph S. Churchill ed., Winston S. Churchill, Companion Vol. II Part 2, 1907-1911 (1969) p.1274.*
8. *Kenneth O. Morgan ed., Lloyd George: Family Letters 1885-1936 (1973) pp.158-59.*
9. *See R. Page Arnot, South Wales Miners Vol. I (1967) pp.185, 205-7; it was Leonard Llewellyn who, as chief manager of the colliery, had refused the miners' offer, a fact confirmed by General Sir Nevil Macready in his memoirs, Annals of An Active Life Vol. I (1924) p.148.*
10. *Churchill ed. (1969) p.1290.*
11. *Marx & Engels, Collected Works Vol. 6 (1976) p.486.*
12. *According to Keith Jeffery and Peter Hennessy, States of Emergency: British Governments and Strikebreaking since 1919 (1983), the armed forces have been deployed – in military or 'civilian' capacities – in the following industrial disputes: railways 1918, 1919, 1955; coal mines 1919 (Yorkshire), 1920, 1921; police 1919 (Liverpool); 40-hours strike 1919 (Glasgow); General Strike 1926; docks 1942 (Tyneside), 1945 (London), 1945, 1947, 1948 (London), 1949, 1950 (London); road transport 1947 (London), 1950 (London); electricity 1949 (London); gas 1950 (London); petrol distribution 1953 (London); shipping 1960 (Western Isles); refuse collection 1970 (Tower Hamlets), 1975 (Glasgow); fire service 1973 (Glasgow), 1977-8; air traffic control 1977 (West Drayton); ambulance service 1979. To these can be added the railway strike (1982) where troops were used in London and the fire service dispute (2002-3).*
13. *Morgan ed. (1973) p.162.*
14. *'Imperialism and the Split in Socialism' in Collected Works Vol. 23 (1964) pp.117-18.*

15. Sidney & Beatrice Webb, *The History of Trade Unionism 1666-1920* (1920) p.750; *Annual Conference Reports of the Independent Labour Party, 1905 and 1910.*

16. *Rhondda Socialist*, April 11, 1912.

17. 'Y Ddraig Goch ynte'r Faner Goch?' (The Red Dragon or the Red Flag?) in *Y Genhinen*, October 1911.

18. *Merthyr Pioneer*, June 17, 1911.

19. Report of Hardie's speech to a Labour Day rally in Tonypandy, in the *Times*, May 2, 1911.

20. *South Wales Press*, October 4, 1911.

21. *Merthyr Express*, October 14, 1911.

22. *Change: A Glamorgan Play in Four Acts* (1913), later translated into Welsh by Magdalen Morgan as *Deufor-Gyfarfod* (1929)

23. Ness Edwards, *The Industrial Revolution in South Wales* (1924); and *The History of the South Wales Miners* (1926)

24. Very little has been published about this aspect of Welsh labour history, and some of that which has contains significant inaccuracies. My own research (provisionally titled 'Labour, Class and Country 1898-1924' for publication in a collection of essays) is intended to help fill this vacuum.

25. Marx & Engels, 'Manifesto of the Communist Party' in *Collected Works* Vol. 6 (1976) p. 503.

26. *South Wales Daily News*, November 12, 1913.

27. *South Wales Daily News*, December 8, 1913.

28. J. R. Raynes, *Engines and Men: the History of the Associated Society of Locomotive Engineers and Firemen* (1921) pp.164-5; Griffiths (2005) pp.61-62.

Index

1990 - Or Llanelly a Hundred Years Hence! 21

Abraham, William ('Mabon') 7, 15, 28, 91
Agadir crisis 38
Amalgamated Society of Railway Servants (ASRS): Taff Vale dispute and judgement 7, 10;
    National All-Grades Programme 9, 11, 12; 1907 crisis and settlement 12-18, 26, 80, 81-82; 'Green
    Book' 13, 99n, 103n; Osborne case 16-17; 1911 railway strike 30, 32, 33, 36-37, 39, 42 and Llanelli
    shootings 60, 70, 73; NUR formation 82
Anti-Socialist Union 91-92
Army regiments: Devonshire 27, 44, 50, 55; Lancashire Fusiliers 27; North Lancashire 43, 55;
    Royal Lincolnshire 53; Royal Lancashire 60; Royal Sussex 52, 53, 55; Welsh 59; Worcestershire 25,
    44-46, 48, 50, 53, 55, 59, 60, 62, 64
Askwith, (Lord) George 14, 32, 36, 38, 100n, 103n, 104n
Asquith, Herbert 16, 17, 32, 36, 71, 72, 80, 81, 87, 91
Associated Society of Locomotive Engineers and Firemen (ASLEF) 11, 12, 14, 27, 30, 32, 33, 36-37, 44,
    75, 80, 82, 97, 98, 100n

Baptists 22, 56, 68
Barnes, George 39, 71
Barry 29, 31,33, 34
Belfast 8, 9, 55, 66, 76
Bell, Richard 13, 100n
Bevan, Jack 42, 43, 49, 76
Brace, William 7, 14, 18
British Socialist Party 95, 100n
Brookes, Dr Arthur 48,75
Burns, John 9, 71, 99n
Buxton, Sydney 30, 32, 36

Cambria Daily Leader 33, 45, 105n
Cambrian dispute (1910-11) 26-29, 41, 88
Campbell, Rev. RJ 7
Campbell-Bannerman, Sir Henry 7, 16, 100n
capitalism 9, 29, 76, 84-85, 91, 93, 94, 98
Cardiff 14, 24, 39, 31, 33, 34, 41, 42, 43, 44, 45, 55, 60
Carmarthen or Carmarthenshire 7, 19, 22, 23, 41, 43, 51, 58, 73, 79
Carter, W. 39, 73
Central Labour College 95
'Change' 94-95
Chartists or People's Charter 20, 96
Chorlton S. 32
Churchill, Winston 17, 76; Cambrian dispute 27-28;
    1911 railway strike 30, 31, 33, 36, 37, 39, 40, 70-71, 72, 88, 89, 104n; Llanelli events 55, 58, 71 and

Harold Spiers 64, 108n; political class role 87-88
Clarion 60-61
Communist Manifesto 83
Copper Works schools 44, 45, 46, 54, 73
Conservative Party, see Tory Party

Dafen 19, 57
Daily Mail 30-31, 103n
Dangerfield, George 8-9, 99n, 103n
Davies, Dr John Lloyd 48
Davies, Dr T. Reginald 54, 105n
Disestablishment, Church 7, 17, 19, 21, 22, 78, 91
dockers or Dockers Union 8, 29, 42, 77, 102n
Dowlais 33, 92-93
Dublin 97

Edward VII, king 14, 21, 22, 88
Edwards, Clement 91
Edwards, J. Hugh 56-57, 91
Edwards, Ness 95
Engels, Frederick 83, 86, 89, 96

Featherstone 70, 76
feudalism 83, 84
First World War, see Great War
Fisher, Ann 52
Fox, Albert 32
Francis, John 47-48
Francis, JO 94
free trade 16, 24, 78
Freeth, Major/Colonel George 27, 45, 60, 73

Gas Workers and General Labourers Union 23
General Railway Workers Union 14, 15, 30, 32, 36-37, 82
George V, king 37, 40, 88
Granet, Sir Guy 30, 36, 38, 103n, 104n
Grayson, Victor 8, 78, 95
Great War 67, 82, 90-91, 100n
Great Western Railway company 10, 17, 18, 19, 29, 30, 34, 43, 50, 57, 68, 69, 76, 98
'Green Book' (1907) 13, 99n, 103n
Griffiths, Dan 41, 77

Haldane, RB 27, 31, 37
Hanbury, Benjamin 47-48
Hardie, James Keir 7, 13, 24; Cambrian dispute 28; 1911 railway strike and agreement 38-40, 58;
     and Llanelli events 58, 66, 70-71, 75, 78, 109n; against Lloyd George 72-73; Dowlais declaration 92-
     93; Welsh nationalism 58, 92-93, 94
Harris, William 52

Henderson, Arthur 38, 71
Hodge, John 23-24, 65
Howard, Sir Stafford 41
Howells, Thomas 57
Hyndman, Henry M.13, 100n

Imperialism - the Highest Stage of Capitalism 84-85, 110n
Independent Labour Party (ILP) 7, 13, 15, 24, 41, 60, 69, 77, 78, 79, 91, 92, 96, 97
Independents, Welsh ('Annibynwyr') 56, 86, 92
Industrial Syndicalist 26, 66
Investiture (1911) 86, 92
Isaacs, Sir Rufus 66

John, John ('Jack') 24-25, 47-49, 62, 68, 73-76, 79, 92-93, 96, 98
John, Walter 53
Jones, Sir David Brynmor 79
Jones, Rev. Hugh 73, 79
Jones, Llwchwr 34-35
Jones, Thomas 43, 44, 51-52, 57, 69
Justice 15

Kellaway, Frederick 76
Killing No Murder! 75-76, 109n

Labour Party 7, 8, 12, 17, 23, 24, 32, 38, 39, 60, 66, 69, 71, 73, 78, 79, 87, 89, 90, 91, 92, 95, 96, 97
Labour Representation Committee 8, 23
Lansbury, George 66, 72
Larkin, Jim 36
Lenin, VI: 1907 railway settlement 15-16; 'trade union neutrality' 16;
    Lloyd George, David 16,90-91; railways and imperialism 84-85
Liberal Party 7, 8-9, 12, 16, 17, 22-24, 26, 28, 33, 41-42, 55, 56, 58, 64, 70, 71, 76, 77, 78, 79, 85, 86, 87, 90-95, 97, 99n
'Lib-labs' 7, 8, 12, 91, 96
Liverpool 29, 30, 32, 55, 56, 66, 67, 70, 76, 97, 110n
Llais Llafur 7-8, 9, 12-13, 14, 96
Llanelli: 1911 strike and shootings 33, 37, 39, 40, 41-49, 59-66, 96, rioting 50-58,
    subsequent controversy 68-80, inquest 62, 73-76; chapels and religion 19, 21, 22-23, 68; choirs 22,
    41; economic and social development 18-19, 21-22, 41; labour movement, development of 7, 18, 23,
    24, 77-79, 95, 97-98; Llanelli Citizens Committee 77-78, 79-80; Llanelli ILP 24, 41,69, 77, 78, 79;
    Llanelli Trades and Labour Council 23, 73, 78; paper boys strike (1911) 77; politics 7, 19-21, 23-24,
    41, 77-79, 95; railway workers 10, 18, 31, 39, 41, 97-98; rugby 24-25; schools strike (1911) 77; Welsh
    language 21, 23
Llanelly and County Guardian 107n
Llanelly Mercury 48, 56, 64-65, 68, 69, 78
Lloyd George, David 7, 8-9, 16, 17, 22, 38, 58, 91; 1907 railway crisis 13,14,16,18,77,87;
    'People's Budget' 16,26; 1911 railway strike 31,36,37,38,55,72,73,76,81,87; English press 55; Keir
    Hardie 38, 72, 73; Lenin 16, 90-91; monarchy 38, 40, 86, 88, 92; political class role 86-91; Welsh
    nationalism 91, 92, 93

Lloyd George, Margaret 37, 38, 73, 88
Llwynypia 27, 31
Lords, Law and House of 7, 8, 16-17, 78
Lowth, Thomas 15, 32

'Mabon' see Abraham, William
MacDonald, J. Ramsay 15, 32, 36, 37, 60, 71, 72, 81, 103n
McKenna, Sir Reginald 76, 79
Macready, General Sir Nevil 27, 31, 64, 73, 89, 110n
Maddison, Fred 13, 100n
Mann, Tom 29, 36, 66, 67
Marx, Karl 83, 86, 89, 96
Masterman, Lucy and Charles 88
Mee, Arthur 21
Merthyr Pioneer 40, 70, 92
Merthyr Tydfil 39, 56, 70, 72, 92
Miners Federation of Great Britain 8, 27, 82, 91
monarchy 86, 88, 89, 92
Moorewood's tinplate mills 24
Morris, Alfred 52

National Union of Railwaymen (NUR) 82, 97, 98
Nevill, Frank 44, 69
New Radnor 59, 63
Newport (Gwent) 12, 17, 20, 24, 29, 31, 33, 42

Oriental Stars Rugby Football Club 25, 73
Old Lodge tinplate works 54
Osborne, WV 16-17

Parfitt, Henry 33, 75
Penygraig 26, 27, 60
'People's Budget' 16, 26
Phillips, J. Lewis 74-75, 79
Phillips, Rev. WF 92
Plant, Joseph 53
Picton Philipps, W 43, 50, 51-52, 69
Pugh, William 42
Pontypool and District Trades and Labour Council 80
Powell-Duffryn company 27

Railway Clerks Association 82
railway companies: see under company name
railway unions: see under union names
railways: capital and investment 10-11, 90; imperialism 84-85; development in south-west Wales 18-19;
    pay and conditions 9-11, 13, 17, 26, 27-28; safety 10; trade unionism 9, 12, 82; nationalisation 12,
    15, 26, 42-43, 93; 1907 crisis and settlement 11-17,18, 26, 32, 37, 87, 90; 1911 strike, deployment
    of military 30, 31, 33, 34, 70-73, 88-89, settlement 37-38; 1911 royal commission 32, 36, 37, 39-40,

membership 71-72, report 80-81
Rees, David 19-21
Rees, DJ 12, 14
religious revival (1905) 8, 24
Richards, Thomas 7, 12, 91
Riot Act (1716) 43, 44, 47, 51, 63, 68, 74
Roberts, Evan 8, 24
Robinson, Sidney 79

Sailors and Firemen, National Union of 29, 36
Seely, Colonel JEB 65, 66
Sharland, Rose 60-61
Shinwell, Emmanuel 36
Social-Democratic Federation 24, 60, 100n, 101n
South Wales Daily News 33, 61-62, 78-79
South Wales Miners Federation 8, 12, 14, 27, 28, 70, 91, 95, 96
South Wales Press 68
South Wales Sentinel and Labour News 77, 78
Spiers, Harold and family 5, 25, 59-67, 108n
Squance, Richard 44, 98
St. Albans Rugby Football Club 24, 25, 73
Stanton, Charles 28-29
Stepney family 19, 41, 52
strikes and industrial disputes: Taff Vale railways (1900) 7; unionisation (1907) 8;
    Powell-Duffryn coal (1910) 27; Cambrian coal (1910-11) 26-29, 41, 88; Trimsaran miners 41;
    seafaring and ports (1911) 29; Miners minimum wage (1912) 27-28, 82; Dublin transport (1913)
    97-98; military deployment in industrial disputes 8, 76, 89 110n, see also 'railways, 1911 strike,
    deployment of military' above
Stuart, Major Brownlow 44, 45, 46, 47, 59, 60, 62, 65, 74-75
Swansea 18, 19, 24, 33, 41, 42, 60, 77, 78, 79, 82
syndicalism 29, 55, 95 see also Industrial Syndicalist

Taff Vale case and railway company 7, 10, 34
Tarian y Gweithiwr 55-56, 58, 96
Thomas, Abel 23, 24, 79
Thomas, DA 7, 26
Thomas, David 92
Thomas, JH 14, 17, 18, 36, 81-82, 88, 98
Thompson, Wilfred 78
Thorne, Will 65, 72
Tillett, Ben 24, 29, 67, 77
tinplate industry 18, 19, 22-24, 54, 57, 73, 97
Tinplate Workers Union of South Wales, Monmouthshire and Gloucestershire 23, 102n
Tonypandy 8, 21, 27, 41, 44, 92
Tories and Tory Party 7, 8, 9, 12, 16, 23, 24, 28, 70, 79, 85-89, 91, 92
Trade Disputes Act (1906) 7, 9
'trade union neutrality' 16, 91
Trades Union Congress (TUC), British 8, 32, 67, 97

Transport Workers, National Federation of 29, 82
Trimsaran 41
Troup, Sir Edward 64, 73, 108n

United Pointsmen's and Signalmen's Society 30, 32, 36-37, 82

Vivian, Frank 78-79

Wales 56-57
Wales, politics in 7-9, 86-87, 89-90, 91-96
Welsh Baptists Union 22
Welsh language 21, 22, 23, 92
'Welsh nationalism' 58, 91-94
Welsh Socialist Republican Movement 96
Western Mail 62
Westminster Gazette 55
Wilkins, Henry 47, 51, 69
Williams, Dr JH 24, 79, 95
Williams, JE 32
Williams, John 7
Williams, Joseph 43, 69
Williams, JE 32
Williams, W. Llewelyn 7, 22-23, 68, 69, 77, 78, 79
Winstone, James 80
Worsell, Leonard 47-48, 68, 73, 75, 76, 77, 79, 96, 98

Y Diwygiwr 20
Y Genhinen 111n
Y Tyst 56, 68

Top: Llanelli demonstration against the shootings, September 1911 (print courtesy of Libraries Department, Llanelli Borough Council)
Bottom: Harold Spiers (the 'deserter') is second from the left, front row, probably 1914 (supplied by Desmond Spiers, Redditch)

Top: The military camp at Burry Port, near Llanelli, August 1911
Bottom: Police and soldiers display damaged provisions, Llanelli, August 1911
(both prints courtesy of Libraries Department, Llanelli Borough Council)

Top:Soldiers of the Royal Sussex Regiment leaving their camp at Burry Port, 1911
Bottom: One of the wrecked railway carriages, Llanelli, August 1911
(both prints courtesy of Libraries Department, Llanelli Borough Council)

212470/
352

30th August, 1911.

Sir,

I am directed by the Secretary to say that he has
noticed in the newspapers the case of a private soldier who
was reported to have refused to fire at Llanelly on the
occasion of the recent riot and who subsequently deserted.
Mr Churchill does not know whether the newspaper reports of
this case are correct and what the special circumstances
may be, but he desires me to say that in his opinion if
the alleged incident actually took place, it would be
contrary to public interest to make the case a cause célèbre
by holding a sensational court martial, thus investing it
with an unnecessary and extremely undesirable importance.
Mr Churchill hopes that the course will be adopted which
will most effectively avoid any undesirable publicity, and
in view of the important bearing the matter has on the
action of the Home Department in dealing with disturbances,
he would be glad to be informed before any decisive step
is taken.

I am,

Sir,

Your obedient Servant,

(Sᵈ) Edward Troup.

The Secretary,

War Office.

Letter from Sir Edward Troup to the War Office, August 30, 1911 (Public Record Office, Kew)

THE DECENT WORKMAN: Here, I'm not having those games put down to me.
Clear off, all of you!
(Cartŵn: Western Mail)

THE TIED-UP RAILWAY SYSTEM
(Cartŵn: Western Mail)

A WISE PRECAUTION
JOHN BULL (picking himself up): Well, after this, I think it is necessary to put
some sort of a kicking-strap on him!
(Cartŵn: Western Mail)

Top left: The Decent Workman: Here, I'm not having those games put down to me. Clear off, all of you! (*Western Mail*, August 1911)

Top right: The Tied-up Railway System (*Western Mail*, August 1911)

Bottom left: A Wise precaution: John Bull (picking himself up after collision with 'Railway Worker' horse): Well, after this , I think it is necessary to put some sort of a kicking-strap on him! (*Western Mail*, August 1911)

Right: The headstones for John John and Leonard Worsell, Box Cemetery, Llanelli, 1981 (photos: Meic Peterson)

IN LOVING MEMORY OF

John H. John,

THE DEAR SON OF W AND M. J. JOHN.

20 RAILWAY TERRACE LLANELLY.

WHO WAS FATALLY SHOT BY THE MILITARY DURING
THE RAILWAY STRIKE. AUG.19.1911 AGED 21 YEARS.

The call was short the shock severe.

To part with one we loved so dear

ALSO MARY J JOHN *HIS MOTHER,*

WHO DIED DEC. 11, 1931. AGED 71 YEARS.

· R · I · P ·

ALSO WILLIAM JOHN *HIS FATHER*

WHO DIED DEC.13 1935. AGED 80 YEARS.

IN

MEMORY OF

LEONARD WORSELL,

WHO WAS FATALLY SHOT BY THE MILITARY
DURING THE RAILWAY STRIKE AUG.19,1911,

AGED 20 YEARS.

ERECTED BY THE LLANELLY TRADES COUNCIL
& LOCAL LABOUR PARTY.

"WORKERS OF THE WORLD, UNITE".

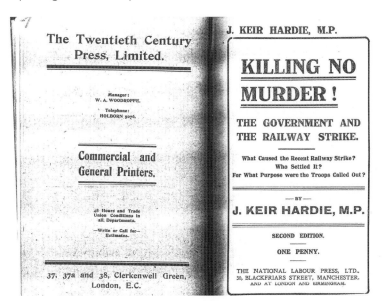

Top: Front and back covers of Keir Hardie pamphlet (1912 edition)
Bottom left: David Lloyd George and Winston Churchill, 1915 *(BBC Hulton Picture Library)*
Bottom right: W. Llewelyn Williams, Liberal MP Carmarthen Boroughs *(Llanelly Mercury1911)*

Top left and top right: John John *(Llanelly Mercury)* and Leonard Worsell *((Llanelly and County Guardian)*, shot dead. Bottom left and right: John Francis *(Llanelly Mercury)* and Ben Hanbury, *((Llanelly and County Guardian)* shot and wounded

James Keir Hardie, Labour MP for Merthyr Boroughs (BBC Hulton Picture Library)